Baseball's Most

Baseball's Most Bizarre Plays

*A Roster of the Odd, the Improbable
and the Downright Confounding
in Major League History*

ALAN HIRSCH

McFarland & Company, Inc., Publishers
Jefferson, North Carolina

ISBN (print) 978–1-4766–8707–0
ISBN (ebook) 978–1-4766–4560–5

LIBRARY OF CONGRESS AND BRITISH LIBRARY
CATALOGUING DATA ARE AVAILABLE

Library of Congress Control Number 2021052794

Front cover image © 2022 zieusin/Shutterstock

Printed in the United States of America

*McFarland & Company, Inc., Publishers
Box 611, Jefferson, North Carolina 28640
www.mcfarlandpub.com*

Table of Contents

Acknowledgments

It takes a village to write a book, at least a book like this. The following villagers all have my heartfelt gratitude for contributing in one way or another: Dan Cohen, the Hirschs (Eric, Joni, Marjorie, Sarah, and Sheldon), Jake Kaden, Joe Markley, Chris Mead, Howard Shapiro, and Brad Whately. The Z boys, Richard Zarin and Rob Zabronsky, went above and beyond.

Preface

When I conceived of a book revolving around the most bizarre plays in baseball history, my college-aged son was skeptical: "Bizarre plays are fun, but who needs to read about them? You can watch them on YouTube." I responded that many of the most bizarre plays predate televised baseball (or television period) and even some of the more recent are not available on YouTube. Moreover, the book would not consist of the amazing plays alone. Rather, each play would inspire commentary—the kind of quirky history and baseball lore that Bill James made famous. My son was confused. "Bill James is the numbers guy, isn't he? What does quirky history have to do with it?"

James has paid the price of genius. Since apparently one can be famous for one thing only, the person with multiple talents often gets cheated when it comes to reputation. You know that Samuel Morse invented the telegraph, right? You may not know that he was a fine painter. So was the immortal poet William Blake. The great Albert Schweitzer was an influential musicologist and one of the leading organists of his day, not to mention a serious theologian. He is remembered primarily for his humanitarian medical work in Africa.

Bill James is indeed a "numbers guy"—the father of sabermetrics (or "analytics"). Because sabermetrics eventually swept major league baseball, it crowded out James' other achievements. Few people realize that James is a preeminent baseball historian. He is an archivist who discovers hidden nuggets, and traffics in the quirky. One example should suffice. James observed uncanny similarities between two baseball players with the same name—the Royals' William "Willie" Wilson and the Mets' William "Mookie" Wilson. That reminded James of an Edgar Allan Poe story about two identical strangers with the same name. The name? William Wilson.

1

Preface

The commentary I offer after each of the 150 bizarre plays is very much in the spirit of Bill James–style baseball history. It involves delicious lore, fun facts, trivia quizzes, improbable connections, controversial opinions, and humorous anecdotes. As for the 150 plays themselves, I must emphasize that they are not the *best* plays in terms of excellence or accomplishment. (Often, they are the opposite.) Babe Ruth makes no appearance in the most bizarre plays, though he of course shows up in the commentary. Lou Gehrig, Robin to Ruth's Batman, makes two appearances, because he happened to be involved in two of the craziest plays of all-time.

You will recognize several of the plays. Yes, Jose Canseco heading a ball over the fence for a home run makes the list. With some reluctance, I also included Randy Johnson blowing up a bird. My reluctance stems less from the gruesomeness of that incident than its fame. All things being equal, I preferred unearthing plays that have not been widely seen, including quite a few from the earlier days of baseball. Unless you are ridiculously knowledgeable, many of these plays will be new to you. Bill James himself might learn a thing or two. Baseball offers a bottomless bag of unbelievable plays.

Some of the most famous plays in baseball history are *literally* unbelievable—they didn't happen. In the course of my research, I found any number of fabulously bizarre plays, some of which were described and presented as real in dozens of books and articles, that never occurred. Or, at a minimum, could not be verified. Once something gets out there, it is guaranteed to be repeated … and repeated and repeated. Urban legends are legion.

One such example will illustrate how I determined whether to include certain alleged plays in my list. In his autobiography, Ty Cobb describes recklessly trying to score from second base on a wild pitch solely because the Boston pitcher, Cy Morgan, covered the plate. Morgan was one of Cobb's many enemies, and Cobb relished the opportunity to spike him or run him over. But when Morgan saw Cobb streaking home with malice, he "turned and actually ran away from the plate."[1] Cobb added that "Morgan was released by Boston that night."[2]

That is such a good yarn that numerous sportswriters have repeated it as fact. It is also potentially verifiable, thanks to Cobb's claim that Morgan was released that night. However, Boston never released Morgan. On June 5, 1909, they *traded* him to Connie Mack's

A's for pitcher Biff Schlitzer and $3,500. Perhaps Cobb simply misremembered, mixing up a release for a trade? Okay, but did Morgan pitch against the Tigers shortly before the Sox traded him? It turns out that Morgan did indeed pitch against Detroit on June 4, the day before he was traded. Moreover, the box score reveals that Cobb scored a run and Morgan uncorked two wild pitches.

So Cobb's scenario seems plausible. True, Morgan was traded the day after the incident allegedly took place, not released that day, but these discrepancies are easily within the margin of memory lapse, especially since Cobb was describing an event from a half-century earlier. And there is a reasonably strong circumstantial case that Cobb did not simply invent this recollection. Is Morgan's June 4 outing against the Tigers, in which he threw a wild pitch and Cobb scored, pure coincidence?

Unfortunately, we do not know. I could find no newspaper or other eyewitness account of the game that reports this incident. Accordingly, I do not include it in the 150 Most Bizarre Plays. Plays that *may* have happened don't make the cut (though, if they are good enough, I find a way of discussing them, as I have here with Morgan's alleged retreat from Cobb's menacing advance). I include the date and relevant details of every play on my list. If I couldn't find the date and details, I sidelined the play. You may or may not agree that my 150 plays are in fact the most bizarre, but you can count on them having happened. And while the verification requirement skews this list toward more recent eras, you will still find on this list plenty of plays way back in time. Well over half of the plays pre-date 2000; roughly one-third predate 1980 and one-fourth pre-date 1960. There are even eight plays from before 1920.

While every sport experiences wacky plays, baseball lends itself to them. It oozes narrative richness. In his book that amounts to an extended love letter to baseball, ESPN's Tim Kurkjian captured this aspect of the sport:

> Baseball is the funniest game because it presents so many opportunities for humor; it has props that other sports don't. It has walls to run into, mounds to run over ... and fans that are nearly in play. In what other sport could Larry Walker toss a baseball to a kid in the stands after making a catch, realize that there were only two out, grab the ball back from the startled child, and throw it to the plate? There is ivy on the outfield fence in Wrigley Field;

Preface

Michael Jordan never had to frantically search for a basketball in the ivy before taking a jump shot. There's a hill in play in centerfield at Houston's Minute Maid Park; Jerry Rice never had to climb a hill to make a catch.... The funniest bloopers come from baseball. The clip of third baseman Lenny Randle on his stomach, *blowing* a bunt into foul territory, will live forever. As will the fly ball that hit right fielder Jose Canseco in the head and bounced over the fence for a home run.[3]

As Kurkjian's examples also illustrate, any list of most bizarre plays will be largely subjective. Which is more bizarre—Lenny Randle blowing a ball foul or Jose Canseco heading a ball over the fence? To some extent, it is just a question of which tickles our funny bone more, and everyone has their own funny bone. But I have employed several criteria. First, is the play unique? If not, how often does it occur? For example, I relish plays at home plate when two runners arrive simultaneously and the catcher tags them both out. Unbelievable! Except, it turns out that has happened at least six times. Accordingly, I've grouped the six plays together and they land in the # 99 spot. Or, to take the example already noted, Lenny Randle blowing a ball foul is something that (believe it or not) happened more than once. All of the plays in the top 20 happened just once and are unlikely to reoccur.

A second criterion is the number of parts involved—meaning players, umpires, bat boys, fans, even inorganic objects. A rundown involving the entire defensive team is presumptively more bizarre than a rundown involving just a few players. The play in which the field announcer (yes, there used to be such a thing) became involved, along with *two* baseballs (yes, that happened too), is unsurprisingly a top ten play.

First and foremost, there is the "can you believe this actually happened?" test. If the answer is no, the play will rank high. All of the Top 25 plays on this list fall into this category. If you don't already know about them, you will half-suspect I'm making them up. Fortunately, as the saying goes, you can look it up.

4

The Plays

150: Down Goes Frazier!

On September 3, 2018, in the second inning, Mets third baseman Todd Frazier tumbled head over heels into the stands after making a spectacular catch of a foul pop lofted by the Dodgers' Alex Verdugo. Umpire Mark Wegner peered into the stands, where Frazier laid sprawled, and determined that the ball remained in Frazier's glove. Batter out. Unbeknownst to Wegner and everyone else (until TV replays exposed the chicanery, too late for Verudgo), Frazier did not have the baseball in his glove: He had a rubber ball that happened to be lying nearby in the stands and that he grabbed after his crash landing. After he emerged from the stands, Frazier tossed the ball back to the crowd, thereby removing the evidence and completing a new version of the hidden ball trick.

COMMENT

Frazier was no stranger to incredible plays. On May 27, 2012, he swung so hard at a pitch by Jamie Moyer that the bat flew out of his hands and toward the mound. Not so unusual except that Frazier made contact before losing his bat and the ball soared over the left-field fence for a home run. And in his first at-bat at Yankee Stadium after his trade to the Yanks in 2017, he grounded into a triple play—made more unusual by the fact that a run scored on the play.

149: Just Like We Practice It

On October 7, 1916, Game 1 of the World Series, the Brooklyn Robins (as they were called before they became the Dodgers), trailing the Red Sox 5–1 in the eighth inning, had a runner on first and Hy Myers at the plate. Myers smashed a ground ball up the middle that pitcher Ernie Shore deflected with his glove hand. The re-directed ball rocketed to shortstop Everett Scott but Scott could not get his glove down in time and the ball struck his ankle. From there it went right to the second baseman Hal Janvrin who was fortuitously stationed near the second base bag. Janvrin stepped on the bag and threw to first for the double-assisted double-play—glove to ankle to glove to glove.

COMMENT

Despite the blow to the ankle, Scott remained in the game and played the rest of the series. And, for that matter, every game over the next eight seasons. He finally missed a game, breaking his consecutive game streak of 1,307, in 1925, the same year Lou Gehrig began his. To this day, only Gehrig and Cal Ripken have surpassed Scott's streak. And yet, Scott played in only 126 and 138 games in 1918 and 1919 respectively. A combination of the Spanish flu and World War I resulted in shortened major league seasons those two years.

Meanwhile, writing in the *Washington Post* the day after the gem involving Scott's ankle, Stanley Milliken observed that "the like of this play has probably never occurred on any ball grounds."[1] The play turned out to be crucial, when the Robins rallied for four runs in the ninth to pull within 6–5. Ernie Shore was relieved by Carl Mays, who gave up a single that loaded the bases before retiring Jake Daubert to end the game and earn a save.

The climactic Mays–Daubert match-up involved two players destined for tragedy before long. Four years later, a pitch by Mays killed Ray Chapman—the only major leaguer ever to suffer a fatal injury during a game. And four years after that, Daubert, in the midst of a reasonably productive season though 40 years old, died of complications after an appendectomy.

148: Tumbling Tommy

On July 10, 2001, in the sixth inning of the all-star game in Seattle, Vladimir Guerrero hacked at a pitch from Mike Hampton, and his splintered bat sailed all the way to the third base coaching box. There stood 73-year-old Tommy LaSorda, an honorary coach for the National League who had actually retired five years earlier but wanted to coach third for the heck of it. As they say, be careful what you wish for. The bat clipped LaSorda's hip and sent him into a cap-losing backwards somersault (that he didn't quite complete).

COMMENT

Hard as it may be to imagine, the roly-poly Lasorda actually pitched in the major leagues. Well, sort of. From 1954 to 1956, he pitched in 26 games amassing a record of 0–4 and an ERA of 6.48, while walking 56 batters in 58 innings. For the record, he came to bat 14 times and scratched out one single, for a batting average of .071. For a ballplayer, Lasorda was a pretty good manager.

It is actually common for successful managers to have been pedestrian players. Leo Durocher was a slick-fielding shortstop who managed to stick around for 17 seasons, during which he hit .222 and managed just 24 home runs. That's downright Ruthian compared to Ralph Houk, who slugged zero home runs in 171 plate appearances spread over eight years as a Yankee. And Houk had a stellar career compared to Walter Alston, who played two innings in the field and came to bat once, in 1936 for the Cardinals. He struck out.

147: Hidden Ball Trick Triple-Play

On April 30, 1929, the White Sox led the Indians 5–3 in the top of the seventh inning. The Tribe threatened, putting Johnny Hodapp at third and Charlie Jamieson at second with no outs. Carl Lind hit a groundball to shortstop Bill Cissell, who threw to first-baseman Bud Clancy for the out. When Clancy saw Hodapp break for home, he threw to catcher Buck Crouse, prompting Hodapp to retreat to third. Crouse fired to third baseman Willie Kamm, who tagged Hodapp for the second out. Meanwhile, Jamieson had cruised into third. As Kamm returned to his position behind the bag, Jamieson took a lead, not suspecting that Kamm had stuffed the ball under his arm. Kamm tagged Jamieson for the third out, and Lind's at-bat officially went down as a triple-play—the only time in major league history that a hidden ball trick produced a tri-killing.

COMMENT

Allegedly Kamm pulled the hidden ball trick another time that season and several times during his career. Ever wonder about the history of the hidden ball trick? Amazingly, baseball historian Bill Deane devoted an entire book (*Finding the Hidden-Ball Trick*) to the subject. Deane reports that the earliest documented hidden ball trick occurred in 1872, and by 1876 it was described as an "old trick."[2]

Kamm's victim on the play, Charles Jamieson, was a superb all-around player but perhaps not the shrewdest base runner. Although known for his speed (he reached double figures in triples three different seasons), that year Jamieson attempted to steal 15 times and was caught 13. The season before, he did a tiny bit better, caught in only 12 of his 15 attempts. But give the man his due. In 1928, the year before Kamm caught him napping, Jamieson was on the other end of two triple-plays, initiating both from the outfield—the only outfielder ever to do so in one season.

146: Mice Play Tag

On August 7, 1954, in the first inning against the Senators, Minnie Minoso of the White Sox tried to score from *first* on a wild pitch that kicked around the backstop. To make matters weirder, when catcher Joe Tipton finally corralled the ball and threw home, the "wrong" Mickey (first baseman Mickey Vernon, not the pitcher Mickey McDermott) was covering home and tagged out Minoso—concluding the adventure of Minnie and the Mickeys.

COMMENT

The play was less of an aberration for Minoso than it would have been for almost anyone else, as he had an adventuresome streak on the bases: He led the American League in stolen bases three times and led the league in caught stealing six times. He also led the league in hit by pitches *ten* times.

Minoso was a legitimate star. The persistence of racism in baseball after Jackie Robinson broke the color barrier in 1947 is apparent from the 1951 Rookie of the Year voting. The award went to Gil McDougald even though Minoso, a black Cuban, easily surpassed McDougald in virtually every statistical category. Minoso deservedly finished fourth in the MVP voting (and McDougald ninth). As Allen Barra has argued, Minoso, who is not in the Hall of Fame, was better than any number of white players who are.[3] Jayson Stark concurs, arguing that Minoso is one of the most underrated plays ever, and makes a compelling case that a movie about his life should be made: "How many guys played in the Cuban Leagues in their teens, in the Negro Leagues in their twenties, in the big leagues in their 50s, and the Northern league in their 70s?"[4]

Admittedly those appearances in his 50s and 70s were public relations stunts enabling Minoso to play in every decade. But his staying power was no gimmick. At the age of 34, Minoso played in all 154 games and led the league in hits, and the following season missed just two games. Then again, Rickey Henderson led the league in stolen bases (66) at the age of 39, also playing in 152 games (though out of 162). But for most impressive longevity, I'd take Julio Franco.

For the five seasons during which he was ages 43–47, Franco's batting average ranged from .273 to .309, he hit 28 home runs, and even stole 19 bases. Unlike Henderson, Minoso, and other late-in-life greats like Stan Musial, Ted Williams, and Carl Yastrzemski, Franco was never a superstar. A statistically typical season for him was 1990 when he batted .296 with 11 home runs in 582 at-bats. A full 14 years later, at the almost unthinkable age of 45, he hit .309 with 6 home runs in only 320 at-bats. The next year, he batted .275 and *increased* his power—swatting nine home runs in 233 at-bats. On May 4, 2007, at the age of 48, Franco homered off Randy Johnson and also stole a base. A full eight years later, as a 56-year-old player-manager in Japan, Franco batted .333 in limited action. Fifty-six-year-olds aren't supposed to see *any* action, except perhaps in slow-pitch softball leagues.

#145: From Toe to Head

On June 16, 1928, the Tigers' Marty McManus smashed a foul ball off his foot. The carnage was only beginning. The ball rolled between shortstop and third, where Senators third baseman, Ossie Bluege and shortstop Bobby Reeves both pursued it, not realizing that the ball had struck McManus and was a dead ball. The two infielders smashed heads, and both went down in a heap.

All three players remained in the game, and Bluege homered to account for the only Senators' run in a 4–1 defeat. The losing pitcher, the man on the mound during the collision, was Bump Hadley, who had a nice name for a pitcher. The nickname (his real name was Irving) stemmed from him contracting the mumps in 1927: He became "Bumps," shortened to Bump.

144: *Where's First?*

On April 26, 1925, the Indians had things well in hand, leading 7–2 with the host White Sox down to their last out. Willie Kamm slapped a grounder to shortstop Joe Sewell, whose throw to first beat Kamm easily. However, first-baseman Ray Knode came off the bag to take the throw (for no apparent reason, if contemporary accounts are to believed, and the official scoring suggests they are) and stumbled around unable to locate the bag. Kamm crossed first, and Knode was credited with an unusual error—failure to find the base. Thousands of White Sox fans who saw the throw to first beat Kamm assumed the game was over and poured on to the field (as used to happen at the end of games, even home team defeats). When the umpires were unable to remove the fans, they had no choice but to declare the game a forfeit. Cleveland won 9–0.

COMMENT

A somewhat similar play occurred on August 7, 1971. The Tigers were one out away from defeating the Red Sox 12–7, though the Sox ninth-inning rally put two men on base for Carl Yastrzemski. Pitcher Fred Scherman induced an easy ground ball to first baseman Norm Cash, and then covered the bag as pitchers are supposed to do. But Cash decided to make the play himself, which would have been fine except Scherman, like a basketball player boxing out an opponent, inadvertently blocked Cash from the bag. Cash couldn't find an opening—his foot never reached the bag, and Yastrzemski reached first with perhaps the most improbable of his 3,419 hits. Tigers manager Billy Martin said, "Never in all my life saw it before."[5] Coach Charlie Silvera suggested to Cash that he "take that play on tour next Winter, and you can make a million bucks with it."[6] (In his first major league game, Silvera hit a triple. During the rest of his ten-year career, he hit one more.)

COMMENT

Eleven years earlier, Cash was involved in one of the most lop-sided trades in baseball history. On April 12, 1960, the Indians dealt him to the Tigers for prospect Steve Demeter. Demeter played four games for the Tribe in '60 (was hitless in five at-bats), was demoted, and spent the next 12 years in the minors before retiring. Cash played 15 seasons with the Tigers, slugging 373 home runs and earning four all-star selections.

The 1925 version of the play beats out the Cash version in 1971 because it led to a forfeit. Forfeits were common in the very early days of the game, usually resulting from riotous fans, interminable arguments by players and managers, or stalling to create a rainout before a game became official. There were generally several such forfeits a year in the 1890s, and a bunch in the first two decades of the twentieth century. But the one caused by Ray Knode's shaky footwork was the only forfeit in 1925 and the last until 1937. The 1937 forfeit almost had significant consequences. The Phils, trailing 8–2 in a not-yet-official game that approached city curfew, stalled relentlessly (holding constant conferences and making frequent pitching changes), leading the legendary umpire Bill Klemm to declare a forfeit in favor of the Cards. That erased the game's statistics, including a Ducky Medwick home run. Medwick ended the season with 31 homers, tying Mel Ott for the league lead—and thus winning the Triple Crown by the thinnest of margins.

The most recent forfeit could have had a far greater impact. On August 10, 1995, with the Dodgers trailing the Cardinals 2–1 in the ninth inning, things went haywire. It was "baseball giveaway" night in Los Angeles, and some inebriated fans had tossed their balls onto the field earlier in the game. When the Dodgers' Raul Mondesi led off the ninth by striking out, he argued and was ejected. As was his manager, Tommy LaSorda. Now fans poured baseballs onto the field. When they couldn't be stopped, umpire Jim Quick called the game in St. Louis' favor. The Dodgers ended up winning their division ... by one game.

#143: Ump Struck

On May 20, 1967, in the fifth inning against the Cardinals in a 4–4 game, the Mets had Jerry Buchek on second and Ron Swoboda at bat with two outs. Swoboda's sharp ground ball was headed for second baseman Julio Javier but it struck umpire Frank Secory, who was on the grass behind the mound, and bounded in the air. Shortstop Dal Maxvill ran down the ball. Having no play on Swoboda, he alertly threw to third, catching Buchek off the bag. Buchek got in a run-down and was eventually tagged out at home to end the inning. Except, after both teams left the field, they were called back on. MLB Rule 509F renders a ball dead when it strikes the umpire prior to passing any player other than the pitcher. Swoboda was credited with a hit and sent to first, and Buchek sent back to third.

COMMENT

Buchek would come in to score, giving the Mets a 5–4 lead. They ended up losing 11–9, squandering a grand slam by their pitcher, Jack Hamilton, the only home run of his eight-year career. On that career, Hamilton batted .107 and struck out 70 times in 150 at-bats. Pathetic as that is, he wasn't close to the worst hitting pitcher of all time. My choice would be Ron Herbel, a decent pitcher with the Giants during the 1960s. From 1964 to 1966, Herbel managed just two hits in 134 at-bats. (He would have had a third, but the poor guy was thrown out at first by right fielder Billy Williams.) For his career, Herbel had six hits (all singles) in 206 at-bats, for a batting average of .029. He struck out 125 times and walked just eight.

One of those walks was notable. Remember Tracy Stallard, who gave up Roger Maris' 61st home run in 1961? He was also the losing pitcher in Jim Bunning's perfect game in 1964, one of Stallard's 20 losses that year. To be fair, someone had to serve up Maris' record-breaking home run and lose against Bunning. And, as is oft remarked, a pitcher has to be pretty good to lose 20 games in a season. In his six-year career, Stallard did only one thing that was truly inexcusable: He walked Ron Herbel with the bases loaded. It was Herbel's second and last RBI of that season. The next year, he added one more. That was it. Herbel pitched nine seasons, came to the plate 227 times, and totaled three RBI—one fewer than Jack Hamilton managed in a single at-bat.

142: A Terrible, Terrific Throw

On August 12, 1981, in the third inning of a scoreless game, the White Sox's Lamar Johnson belted a ball high off the Green Monster in Fenway Park. As often happens with the monster, Johnson thought double, took a wide turn, but had to scramble back to first when he saw Jim Rice retrieve the ball quickly. Rice's throw, however, sailed way over the head of second baseman Jerry Remy and carried all the way to first baseman Tony Perez, who tagged out Johnson—an accidental assist on a dreadful throw.

COMMENT

Later in the game Rice added an intentional assist, throwing out fellow future Hall of Famer Carlton Fisk trying to stretch a single into a double. On the play in which Rice recorded the accidental assist, Ron LeFlore scored what turned out to be the only run against Sox hurler Bobby Ojeda. Five years later, Ojeda was the beneficiary of an exceptionally lucky trade. Prior to the 1986 season, the Red Sox traded him to the Mets. As a result, he played on a miraculous World Championship team instead of the team that suffered a heartbreaking defeat.

Then again, had the Sox kept Ojeda, perhaps they would have won rather than lost the 1986 World Series. He pitched a complete game victory for the Mets in Game 2 and was their no-decision starter in the infamous Game 6 Sox collapse. But this gets complicated. In the trade for Ojeda, the Sox received reliever Calvin Schiraldi. Schiraldi was on the mound for the Game 6 collapse, but he had a terrific regular season: Called up mid-season, he recorded nine saves and an ERA of 1.41. Perhaps the Red Sox would not have won the pennant without him. On the other hand, Ojeda was 18–5 with a 2.57 ERA for the Mets, though it is unlikely he would have fared so well as a southpaw in Fenway. In any case, the trading of Ojeda was not quite as bad as the Sox selling another pretty good left-handed pitcher, Babe Ruth, to a New York team.

141: Lucky Bucky Comes Home

On August 13, 1925, in the fourth inning the Indians had Tris Speaker on third and Joe Sewell at second. George Burns hit a ground ball to second baseman Bucky Harris. Speaker broke for home but Harris' throw had him beat easily, forcing Speaker into a rundown. Harris charged home to assist in the rundown. Lo and behold, he took the throw from third baseman Ossie Bluege and tagged Speaker out at the plate. Harris thus had an assist and putout on the same play— hardly unique for a second baseman, except when the putout is at home plate.

COMMENT

It is perhaps not surprising that Bucky Harris, of all people, made such a heads-up play. He was player-manager that season, and had a 29-year career as a manager after his playing days. Despite his sub .500 record, Harris was inducted into the Hall of Fame as a manager. Perhaps he deserved it as a Red Sox *general* manager, since he signed the first African American in the team's history more than a decade after Jackie Robinson broke the color barrier. On the other hand, that player, Pumpsie Green, did not amount to much.

George Burns, the man who hit into the all-Harris double-play, batted .307 over 16 seasons and played on two World Series champions: the Indians in 1920 and A's in 1929. However, to call Burns a contributor in the '29 series would be overly generous. The 36-year-old came to bat twice in the series, both in the seventh inning of Game 4. The A's, trailing 8–0, scored ten runs in the inning, for an amazing come-from-behind win. Burns popped out to make the first out of the inning and struck out to end it. In an inning in which the A's sent 15 men to the plate, Burns went 0–2. If it weren't for him, the A's might still be batting.

140: Routine Fly-Ball Home Run

On June 23, 1940, in the eighth inning of the first game of a doubleheader against the Red Sox, the Indians' Ray Mack lofted a fly that could have been caught by either leftfielder Ted Williams or centerfielder Doc Cramer. However, Williams and Cramer engaged in a full-speed collision that knocked Williams unconscious and broke his jaw. With the two outfielders grounded, Mack cruised around the bases for an inside-the-park home run.

COMMENT

Two runs scored on the play, leading the Tribe past the Sox and Lefty Grove, 4–1. However, in the second game of the doubleheader, the Red Sox prevailed 2–0 thanks to the only shutout of Herb Hash's brief career. Both Red Sox runs were supplied by Jim Tabor home runs. Tabor, who had a pedestrian career (.270 lifetime batting average and 104 home runs), occasionally had days like that. The year before, he hit only 14 home runs, but four came on a single day—a July 4 double-header that saw him drive in 11 runs, including *grand slams on consecutive at-bats.*

139: Foul Play

On May 23, 1966, the Dodgers and Pirates were tied 2–2 in the bottom of the ninth, with the Dodgers' Jon Roseboro on second and two out. Pinch-hitter Derrell Griffin topped a ground ball down the first base line but at least three feet foul—so far foul that Griffin barely ran and the Pirates infielders barely moved. Suddenly the ball kicked fair, and pitcher Pete Mikkelsen, catcher Jerry May, and first baseman Donn Clendenon all raced to it. Mikkelsen grabbed the ball but his sweep tag just missed Griffin. Meanwhile, the Pirates were so mesmerized by the magical hit that no one covered home, leaving Roseboro to gallop in for the walk-off win.

COMMENT

Dodgers manager Walter Alston called the play the strangest he had seen in his 30 years in baseball.[7] Just nine months earlier, Roseboro was involved in an infamous incident, when Juan Marichal clobbered him over the head with a bat. It is widely known that the escapade occurred when Roseboro's throw back to pitcher Sandy Koufax grazed Marichal's ear—or at least came close enough so that Marichal turned and snapped at Roseboro. The catcher emerged with fists clenched, and Marichal whacked him over the head with his bat twice.

According to John Rosengren's intriguing book about the incident, Marichal and Roseboro were on edge for reasons unrelated to baseball.[8] The episode occurred against the backdrop of the Watts riots (less than two weeks earlier) near Roseboro's Los Angeles home and a civil war in the Dominican Republic, Marichal's native country.

Incidentally, while Marichal wasn't quite the greatest pitcher of all-time, he was the greatest against the greatest—in eight all-star games, he gave up just one earned run in 18 innings, and allowed just nine base runners. On the opposite end of the spectrum, in 16 all-star games, Mickey Mantle batted .233 and struck out 17 times in 43 at-bats. Not a shock, given that to Mick, "the all-star game was mostly a cocktail party."[9]

138: Ball on Wall

In the third inning of a Yankees–Red Sox game on July 4, 2008, Kevin Youkilis lofted a long fly to left and Johnny Damon (then a Yankee) almost made a great leaping catch. However, the ball slipped out of Damon's glove and rested on the top of the wall. An alert fan could have blown it back on to the field. An acrobatic fan might have blown it the other way for a home run. Meanwhile, with Damon lying prone, hurt by his collision with the wall, the ball finally rolled down onto the field. Damon heroically got up and held Youkilis to a triple. Then Damon came out of the game and onto to the disabled list for the only time in his 14-year career.

COMMENT

Despite the stint on the DL, Damon played in 143 games that year—one of 16 consecutive seasons in which he played 140 games or more. His remarkable durability is further illustrated by his playing 150 games in 2011 at the age of 38. To give some basis for comparison, consider the other man who figured in the play, Damon's one-time teammate Kevin Youkilis. Youk played in 140 or more games only three times.

Youkilis was made famous by *Moneyball*, which portrayed him as a non-athletic player with an uncanny ability to reach base. More specifically, Michael Lewis dubbed him "the Greek God of Walks" while characterizing him as "a fat third baseman who couldn't run, throw, or field."[10] It may come as a surprise, then, that Youkilis has the second highest fielding percentage for first-baseman in major league history, and only once finished in the top ten in the league in walks. Oh, and he isn't Greek.

137: *Game of Inches*

On June 15, 1947, the Dodgers had the bases loaded against the Cardinals in the eighth inning: Eddie Stanky on third, Al Gionfriddo on second, and Jackie Robinson on first: Carl Furillo hit a high fly ball off the top of the right-field pavilion that bounded back onto the field. Stanky cruised home but Gionfriddo, waiting to see if the ball would be caught, stopped at third and created a logjam—Robinson was on his heels between second and third and Furillo not far behind at second. Seeing Gionfriddo hold up, Robinson retreated to second and Furillo to first. However, when the relay home from second baseman Red Schoendienst got away from catcher Del Rice, Gionfriddo sped home. Rice recovered the ball and threw to pitcher Howie Pollet who tagged Gionfriddo out at the plate. By now Robinson had returned to third and Furillo to second—no doubt exhausted and with relatively little to show for it.

COMMENT

Furillo was credited with a single (reaching second on a fielder's choice) and one RBI, after missing a grand slam by inches. Gionfriddo, the culprit on the play, had an exceptionally strange career arc. Everyone knows about his great catch in Game 6 the 1947 World Series robbing Joe DiMaggio of an extra base hit. Gionfriddo also scored the tying run in the ninth inning of the Dodgers' Game 4 win. Although it was only his fourth season in the big leagues, and first with the Dodgers, and though he was just 25, Game 6 was the last game Gionfriddo ever played in the major leagues. The Dodgers rewarded his World Series heroism by sending him to Triple A, and he played six more seasons in the minors before retiring. His first season back down, in 1948, he hit .294, had a superb on-base percentage of .392, and smacked 25 home runs in 432 at-bats. Even apart from his World Series heroism the previous year, which presumably created some good will, it is a wonder he was never brought up. Though the Dodgers' outfield was stacked, you would think they could have found a willing trading partner if nothing else. Instead, Gionfriddo languished in the minors for the duration of his career. You could look at him as a marginal player who enjoyed World Series glory or a pretty darned good player who, despite the World Series glory, was mysteriously discarded.

The Dodgers treated Furillo even more shabbily, releasing him early in 1960 while he was injured, in order to avoid paying his medical expenses and the higher pension he would have earned as a 15-year player. Furillo successfully sued the organization. The Dodgers argued that he was washed up, but while he was 38, in each of the two previous seasons Furillo batted .290. The Yankees and Dodgers, the two most storied franchises in baseball history, were not known for their generosity.

136: Motley Crew

This play bears uncanny similarities to the previous play. On April 21, 1985, in the top of the 13th inning against the Tigers, the Royals loaded the bases for Darryl Motley. Motley's long drive to right center hit the top of the screen, missing a grand slam by inches. Instead of the four runs, the Royals managed just one. George Brett, who started the play at second, stayed on the bag to tag up. Bad move. Brett was thrown out at the plate. Hal McCrae, who started the play at first, was held up by Brett, and ended up at second, where Motley joined him. McCrae screamed at Motley to return to first, which he did, but not without first colliding with the Tigers shortstop Alan Trammell.

COMMENT

Could things get worse for a team that just scored one run instead of four by the margin of a few inches? Well, in the bottom of the 13th, the Tigers loaded the bases with two outs. Kirk Gibson lofted a high foul into third base territory that Brett camped under. Having just committed a base-running blunder in the top of the 13th, Brett dropped what would have been a game-ending catch. I don't know if Brett is superstitious, but he surely suffered one of the worst 13th innings in baseball history. Gibson, who would achieve immortal glory several years later for his World Series home run again Dennis Eckersley, failed to take advantage of Brett's gift, bouncing out to first. The Royals prevailed despite Brett's meltdown.

Any mention of George Brett in connection with a meltdown evokes the Pine Tar game on July 24, 1983, when Brett's game-winning home run off Goose Gossage was nullified because of Brett's technically illegal bat. Upon the umpire signaling him out, Brett exploded out of the dugout as if shot from a cannon. Incidentally, the box score of that game indicates something bizarre—the appearance of Yankees ace, Ron Guidry, in centerfield. Huh? When the game was completed on August 18, 1983, after American League president Lee MacPhail overruled the umpires and allowed Brett's home run, Yankees manager Billy Martin protested by putting a pitcher in the outfield. A strange protest by a strange manager.

Fun fact about Brett: Immediately after achieving his 3,000th base hit, he was picked off first base.

135: It's the Little Things

On September 3, 2001, the Mets and Phils were tied at 7 in the top of the ninth. Todd Zeile, on second, was the potential go-ahead run, with Robin Ventura at bat against Jose Santiago. Annoyed by a ball call on a 2–2 pitch, Santiago took his eye off the throw back from catcher Todd Pratt. The ball deflected off Santiago's glove and rolled to shortstop Jimmy Rollins. Zeile raced to third, and Rollins' wild throw there allowed him to score. The official scorer charged Santiago with an error for allowing Zeile to reach third and Rollins an error for allowing him to score. Two errors beginning with a catcher's toss to the mound allowed the game-winning run to score.

COMMENT

It certainly wasn't Zeile's blinding speed that made the play. In eleven different seasons, he stole exactly one base (and swapped zero bags on four other occasions). Speaking of the number eleven, that's how many teams Zeile played for—the fifth most in major league history. And he had 11 straight seasons hitting ten or more home runs.

Ventura, who was almost Zeile's equal for consistent power (hitting ten or more homers in 13 out of 14 seasons), is better known for more unusual successes and failures: He is the only player ever to hit grand slams in both games of a doubleheader, and was outpointed by Nolan Ryan in what ESPN's SportsCenter ranked the top baseball brawl of all-time.

134: A Dangerous Walk

On July 30, 2014, in the sixth inning the Pirates, leading 5–4, had Gaby Sanchez on third base and Travis Snider on second with one out against the Giants. Chris Stewart drew a walk to load the bases. Snider, however, mistakenly thinking the bases were already loaded before Stewart walked, started jogging towards third. The Giants caught him in a rundown and tagged him out. Sanchez decided to take advantage of his teammate's blunder and broke for the plate, where he was easily thrown out to end the inning. The Pirates had second and third with one out, and drew a walk that turned into an inning ending double-play.

COMMENT

It went down as caught stealing for Snider—his only caught stealing in 140 games that year. (Then again, it was one of only two attempts, if you could call it that.) The play bears similarity to one that would be high on the Most Bizarre Plays list if it could be verified. Allegedly in a game in 1906, Pittsburgh's Fred Clarke, stole home *accidentally* when he, along with the catcher and everyone else, believed the batter had walked, forcing him in from third. In fact (at least as legend has it), the umpire had called the pitch a strike, but gone momentarily speechless. Clarke strolled across the plate, with a leisurely, uncontested theft of home. However, I find no contemporary account confirming the play.

Clarke could steal home without umpire confusion and defensive indifference. His 15 career swipes of the plate puts him in a tie for 18th in baseball history. Ty Cobb is the easy leader with 54. You may be surprised to learn that Lou Gehrig stole home 15 times, and Babe Ruth 10. But, if the alleged play happened, Clarke is the undisputed champion of *accidental* steals of home. A Hall of Fame outfielder and manager, he also holds another distinction that has lasted 125 years (and counting): the best debut in major league history. In his first game, in 1894, Clarke stroked five hits in five at-bats.

One player to almost match that achievement was John Paciorek. In 1963, as an 18-year-old playing for the Houston Colts, Paciorek came to the plate five times and reached base all five—three base hits and two walks. But while Paciorek and Clarke began their careers almost identically, their career arcs dramatically diverged thereafter. Clarke played in 2,246 games over 21 seasons. Paciorek never played in another game (thanks to spinal fusion surgery). He goes down in the record book as the only player with over two at-bats to enjoy a career batting average, on-base percentage, and slugging percentage of 1.000.

Another noteworthy baseball figure, whose career splits the difference between Clarke and Paciorek, shared their brilliance in his debut. On September 17, 1912, one Charles Dillon "Casey" Stengel reached base five times in his first game, with four hits and a walk along with two stolen bases. He later observed: "I broke in with four hits and the writers promptly decided they had seen the new Ty Cobb. It took me only a few days to correct that impression."[11] Stengel's playing career landed in between Clarke's and Paciorek's: He lasted 14 years but as a regular in only half of them—a singles hitter with modest speed. Successful manager, though.

133: *The Supreme Sacrifice*

On July 4, 1976, with the Cubs leading the Mets 2–1 in the seventh inning and seeking an insurance run, pitcher Ray Burris tried to sacrifice Mick Kelleher to second. Burris bunted back to the mound where pitcher Mickey Lolich fielded the ball, glanced at second, and opted for the safe out at first. However, Lolich's throw sailed ten feet over the head of first baseman Mike Phillips. By the time gangly right fielder Dave Kingman retrieved the ball, Kelleher was rounding third and heading home. Kingman's wild throw got past Jerry Grote and landed in the Cubs dugout, allowing Burris to score as well—on his own sacrifice bunt.

COMMENT

Kingman went 0–4 with three strikeouts in the game, extending his hitless streak to 18. That was not an unusual game for Kingman, a challenged defensive player and one of the great all-or-nothing hitters of all time. That season, he blasted 37 home runs in just 474 at-bats—a superb rate of a home run every 13 at-bats. But he struck out 135 times, an almost obscene rate of a strikeout every 3.16 at bats. Then again, Kingman may have been decades ahead of his time—more concerned with launch angles (though he probably wouldn't have used that terminology) than making contact. Whereas Kingman was maligned for striking out so much, today's sluggers, bolstered by the discovery by the analytics folks that home runs are underrated and strikeouts overrated, are comfortable taking the all-or-nothing approach at the plate.

As for Lolich, Kingman's partner in crime on the play, the mishap was weirdly characteristic for him that year. It was one of his six errors in 1976, the most in his 16-year career. Indeed, in the previous season and subsequent two seasons combined, he pitched in 79 games without committing a single error.

132: Back to Back

In the fourth inning on September 4, 2009, when Reds pitcher Bronson Arroyo spun around after his delivery, Yunel Escobar's line drive struck him squarely in the back. Arroyo pounced on the ball and fired to first, but his throw hit Escobar ... in the back. Pay*back*? To make the play weirder still, Escobar was ruled out for running in fair territory, a rare occurrence. And he twisted his ankle on the first base bag and had to be removed from the game—injury added to insult.

COMMENT

The Reds won 3–1, with Arroyo outdueling Derek Lowe, his teammate on the 2004 Red Sox World Series championship team. In that series, Arroyo was involved in a more famous play: Alex Rodriguez's karate chop knocking the ball out of his glove during Game 6. (A-Rod was called out, and hilariously protested that he was innocently running the bases and did nothing wrong.) The play raises provocative questions about sportsmanship. The Red Sox were infuriated by A-Rod's bush-league move. Some anonymous Yankees agreed. But suppose the play succeeded. Think the Yankees would have regretted winning the game? After the incident, Curt Schilling said that A-Rod wasn't a true Yankee like Derek Jeter, Mariano Rivera and Bernie Williams. Wait a minute: Isn't that the same Derek Jeter who feigned agony after not being hit by a pitch in order to fool the umpire into awarding him first base? How about the time A-Rod, running the bases, screamed "I got it" and caused Blue Jays third baseman Howie Clark (mistaking A-Rod for Jays shortstop John McDonald) to let the ball drop? A brilliant play or bush league? A lot of people said the latter, but surely many of them would have felt differently if the "culprit" was Jeter rather than A-Rod. Things would be clearer if baseball's so-called unwritten rules were written.

131: *Maldonado Rips Cover Off Ball*

On April 18, 2014, with one out in the sixth inning, the Brewers' Martin Maldonado bounced a groundball to Pirates third baseman Pedro Alvarez. Maldonado reached safely when Alvarez's throw died out of his hand and seven-hopped its way to first baseman Gaby Sanchez. It looked like something was off and it turned out something was literally off: the cover of the baseball. When a batter smashes a home run, we sometimes say he ripped the cover off the baseball. Maldonado's routine ground ball did exactly that.

COMMENT

Divine intervention or natural disaster was needed for Maldonado to leg out an infield hit. To say he runs like a catcher is unfair to catchers: Maldonado managed two stolen bases and three triples in a nine-year career. Conversely, Alvarez struggled defensively even without a defective baseball: That season he led National League third basemen in errors with 25, despite playing only 99 games. In each of the two previous seasons, he led National League third basemen in errors with 27. After 2014, his third consecutive error-filled season at the hot corner, the Pirates moved Alvarez to first base. He proceeded to make 23 errors, again leading the National League for players at his position. In 2016, however, Alvarez committed only four errors, as his new team, the Orioles, found the right position for him: designated hitter. (Those four errors came in just 12 games at third base, before the Orioles wisely decided to retire his glove.)

130: *In-Vince-ible*

In the second inning against the Phillies on June 30, 2018, the Nationals' Adam Eaton smashed a line drive off the forearm of right-handed pitcher Vince Velasquez. Velasquez reacted oddly, throwing his mitt to the ground as he chased down the ball on the third-base side of the mound, then making a perfect throw *left-handed* to nip Eaton. Why? Because the line drive injured his right arm. Velasquez left the game immediately after his brilliant play.

COMMENT

Velasquez's ability to throw hard with his left hand is maybe not shocking: He batted .608 as a switch-hitter his junior year in high school. Think he is a good athlete? In an extra-inning game in 2019, Velasquez entered the game in left field when the Phillies, out of pitchers (he had started two days earlier and thrown a bullpen that day), were forced to use outfielder Roman Quinn on the mound. Playing his unaccustomed position, Velasquez threw a runner out at the plate to save the game and later made a diving catch. His lifetime batting average of .224 surpasses that of some position players.

Velasquez's ability to hit raises a question one sometimes hears: Shouldn't National League pitchers work on their hitting? The answer is not necessarily. Because pitchers bat at the bottom of the order, and rarely last into the eighth inning, and often bunt, they simply don't get enough at-bats for their hitting to be very important. Velasquez himself has never had more than 40 at-bats in a season. Imagine he hits .224 (his career average) over 40 at-bats. Now suppose he were a more typical pitcher and hit 75 points less. That would amount to four fewer hits spread over 30 games. In the practice time it would take a pitcher to raise his average 75 points, he would probably be better off working on his pick-off move or defense.

129: Security Crisis

On June 7, 2019, with Anthony Rizzo on first against the Cards in the fifth inning, Kris Bryant's base hit down the third base line and into foul territory in left field struck a security guard. Left fielder Marcell Ozuna threw up his hands to indicate that play should stop. Figuring he might as well keep running in case Ozuna was mistaken, Rizzo headed home. Belatedly making a similar calculus, Ozuna ran down and picked up the ball and threw a strike to home plate, just in time to get Rizzo. Lucky for him, since a ball that hits a security guard remains in play. Rizzo was out despite a heads-up play and Ozuna was rewarded for his own folly.

The Plays

COMMENT

The relevant rule is 6.01(d), unintentional interference, which establishes that when personnel authorized to be on the field (this includes ball boys and ball girls as well as security personnel) unintentionally interfere with a play, the ball remains live. The baseball rulebook, like the U.S. Constitution, is a brilliant document marred by some dubious provisions. In an oft-cited blogpost, Grant Brisbee proposed that baseball's dumbest rule is the one allowing a runner to reach first base on a third strike not caught by the catcher.[12] Typically, this involves the batter swinging at a wayward pitch—why reward him? The misstep by the pitcher or catcher will be punished if there are base runners, but why allow the *batter*, who struck out, to benefit? He's got a point.

My candidate for dumbest rule is sort of related: The batter credited with a base hit when his batted ball strikes a runner who is not touching any base. The runner is declared out while the batter takes first base. That part of the rule makes sense, but why is the batter credited with a base hit? The result of the play is similar to a force out, which of course counts against a player's batting average. I understand the idea that one should not presume that the ball would have been fielded and the batter thrown out, but why presume that he would have reached base? Why not make no assumptions, and treat the play (for scoring purposes) like a hit batter or catcher's interference, neither of which affects batting average?

This may not seem terribly important, but tell that to the pitcher who gets cheated out of a no-hitter by this odd rule. Apparently that hasn't yet happened, which leaves a few candidates for the most painful near no-hitters of all time. Harvey Haddix's 12-inning perfect game, in which he lost everything (perfect game, no-hitter, and ballgame) in the unlucky 13th? Maybe Rich Hill, the Dodger pitcher whose perfect game in 2017 was lost to a teammate's error in the ninth inning before Hill gave up a walk-off home-run in the tenth to cost him everything else?

By the way, the dubious rule allowing a batter to reach base on a strikeout means that a pitcher can get four (or more) strikeouts in an inning. This has happened plenty in the regular season but just once in a World Series (1908), by an unsung pitcher with one of the great unsung names in baseball history: Orval Overall.

25

128: Out of Line

On April 6, 2013, in the seventh inning the Marlins tied the game against the Mets 3–3 when Juan Pierre scored from second on Greg Dobbs' single to right. Mike Baxter's throw home sailed 10 feet wide of the plate on the first base side where catcher John Buck raced to snag it. Pierre's momentum took him toward Buck, who by now was poised to try to throw out Dobbs as he headed for second. Pierre collided with and upended Buck. The umpire called interference on Pierre, and therefore ruled Dobbs out at second. Yes, a runner who had already scored caused an out by interfering with a catcher nowhere near home plate.

COMMENT

Speaking of things that happened only once (if at all), a player once allegedly registered an inside-the-park home run when the ball he smacked to deep center rolled into a doghouse that for some reason stood at the base of a flag pole in the outfield. Unable to retrieve the ball by reaching in, center fielder Socks Seybold poked his head in the doghouse, where it (his head, that is) got stuck. The batter circled the bases for a unique home run.

That play doesn't make the 150 Most Bizarre Plays list because I have been unable to verify that it actually happened. If it did, Seybold gave new meaning to the idea of a player in the doghouse. Usually, players find their way into the manager's metaphorical doghouse. On at least two occasions, a manager's doghouse had a significant impact on the post-season—in one case perhaps proving decisive in the most ballyhooed game in baseball history. We'll save that one for last. First, the 1927 World Series in which the Yankees swept the Pirates with an assist from the manager's doghouse.

One of the Pirates' best players, Kiki Cuyler, batted .309 and posted an on-base percentage of .394 during the regular season. But throughout the season, Cuyler and Pirates manager Donnie Bush butted heads. Bush fined and benched the star outfielder for failing to break up double-plays and hit the cut-off man. Cuyler hardly played in August and September. Rumor has it that Bush wanted Cuyler in the lineup during the World Series but in the number two spot in the lineup, not Cuyler's accustomed three spot: The superstitious Cuyler hated the number two and allegedly refused. All we know for sure is that one of the Pirates' best players, though healthy, did not see the field in the entire series. Two of the Yankees' wins were by one run. It is quite possible that Cuyler would have made a difference.

Pirates fans certainly thought so. The *New York Times* account of Game 2, a 6–2 Yankees win, noted that the fans waged a remarkable demonstration in protest :

> In the eighth inning today, when a pinch hitter was needed, the fans rose by the thousands and set up a deafening clamor for Cuyler. But Donnie Bush was obdurate and called on Earl Smith, and the storm of boos and jeers and catcalls would have done credit to St. Louis.... When Smith grounded weakly to Gehrig another chorus of derisive jeers and laughter greeted the failure of Cuyler's substitute.

Many Brooklyn Dodgers fans felt the same way in 1951, after Bobby Thompson's "Shot Heard Round the World" off Ralph Branca in a playoff game won the Giants the pennant. Clem Labine and Carl Erskine were also warming up in the Dodgers' bullpen when manager Charlie Dressen opted to bring in Branca to face Thompson. At the Baseball Writers Association's annual dinner after the season, Brooklyn writers performed a song they had written: "Turn back the hands of time/Where oh where was Clem Labine?/Give me that lead that once was mine/And let's do it all over again." (Four years later, after Labine's brilliant season helped the Dodgers win the 1955 World Series, Brooklyn writers sang: "Oh my darlin,' oh my darlin,' oh my darlin' Clem Labine.")

Where was Clem Labine? A good question considering his performance after he was called up mid-season in '51. He was 5–1 with a 2.20 ERA in 14 appearances (including six starts), and had just shut out the Giants in Game 2 of the three-game playoff. But that means Labine would have been pitching two days after hurling a complete game. That may explain why Labine wasn't summoned on October 3, but it leads to a more vexing question: Where oh where was Clem Labine the previous two weeks while the Dodgers collapsed and the Giants tied them to force the playoff? Answer: He was in Charlie Dressen's doghouse.

On the next to last weekend of the regular season, Labine started against the Phillies. With the bases loaded in the first inning, he threw his first pitch to Willie "Puddin' Head" Jones from the stretch. Dressen raced to the mound and instructed the rookie to use the full wind-up. Labine stubbornly stuck with the stretch, and Jones creamed a grand slam. Dressen lifted Labine the next inning, and didn't pitch him again for eleven days. That included two games in which Labine was listed as "probable starter." The Dodgers lost both of those games and saw their once seemingly insurmountable 13.5 game lead over the Giants disappear. In his excellent book about that season, Joshua Prager quotes Labine as saying that Dressen "was a very vindictive person."[13]

As an aside (far aside), Puddin' Head Jones got his nickname from a Frankie Valli song by that name about a "fat and funny" boy whose lack of intelligence leads the cruel boys to call him "Woodenhead." But Woodenhead, Puddin' Head Jones laughs last. He marries the teacher they all fancy and survives the Great Depression because he is too ignorant to invest the money he made at his menial job.

127: Sorry, No One's Home

Numerologists will appreciate this one. On 5/5/65 (too bad it wasn't 1955), can you guess the score of the Giants and Cardinals after nine innings? 5–5, of course. And when the Giants broke the game open in the tenth, guess how many runs they scored? Yep, five. With the benefit of a mighty strange play.

With Tom Haller on first base and Jim Davenport on third, one out and the game still tied, Ed Bailey slapped a groundball to Cardinals second baseman Phil Gagliano. Gagliano booted the ball, costing him the chance of an inning-ending double-play. But rather than settling for the out at first, he fired home trying to nab Davenport. Just one problem: No one was covering home. Catcher Bob Uecker had flown down the first-base line to back up what he assumed would be a throw to first to complete the double-play. Good hustle perhaps, but catchers are not supposed to leave home plate vacant with a runner on third. Gagliano's throw sailed to the backstop, and the Giants suddenly led 6–5 with runners on second and third.

COMMENT

Gagliano was charged with two errors on the play, whereas Uecker escaped unscathed. Abandonment of home plate is not considered an error.

Uecker achieved fame as a marginal player with a devoted fan club, not to mention a great sense of humor. He actually homered in the game in question (off Hall of Famer Gaylord Perry)—one of just two round-trippers he hit that year. Uecker never played in more than 80 games in a season and batted .200 lifetime, but lasted six years in the big leagues because he was an excellent defensive catcher. Indeed, the defensive blunder involved *two* players who were in the big leagues for their defense. Gagliano was a lifetime .238 hitter who, in a long career, hit just 14 home runs—the exact total as Uecker. On the play in question, the chance of a double-play was high: The batter, Bailey, and runner on first, Haller, were both slow-footed catchers. This play was full of slow-footed catchers: Uecker (whom I half-jokingly said had "flown" down the line to back up first) had *zero* stolen bases and triples in his career.

126: El Mago's Magic Wand

On April 8, 2019, with two Cubs on base and two outs in the second inning against the Pirates, Javier Baez faced an 0–2 count. James Taillon fooled Baez badly on a curve ball that bounced in front of the plate and well wide of the outside corner, inducing Baez to throw his bat at the ball. The thrown bat met the bouncing ball and the synergy produced a bloop single that scored a run.

COMMENT

What are the odds of throwing the bat and getting a base hit? One in 1,000? Supposing the prospect of getting a base hit on a pitch that bounces is also one in 1,000, the chance of combining the two, and producing a base hit by throwing the bat at a bouncing ball, is one in one million. It is fitting that the player who accomplished this feat is nicknamed El Mago (the Magician). The magic consisted of Baez combining the two parts—thrown bat and bounced ball. Each part alone has been achieved a number of times. Several batters have gotten base hits on thrown bats, and Corey Dickerson actually has *two doubles* on bounced pitches.

Not surprisingly, Vladimir Guerrero, a notorious bad-ball hitter, also managed a base hit on a bounced pitch. On August 14, 2009, in the top of the first against the Orioles, Vlad swung at a pitch by Chris

Tillman that bounced a foot in front of home plate. Guerrero hit it like a cricket shot and looped a base hit to left. As Vlad rounded first, left fielder Felix Pie air-mailed the ball all the way to the first-base dugout, allowing Guerrero to reach second. That game was odd all-around. The Orioles scored a touchdown (seven runs) in the seventh to win by a touchdown and a field goal (16–6). To atone for his first-inning error, Pie hit for the cycle.

125: To No A(Vail)

On August 14, 1979, during a nightmarish fifth inning in which the Giants scored seven runs, Cubs outfielder Mike Vail dropped a routine fly-ball off the bat of Larry Herndon. Vail thought he had time to recover and catch Mike Ivie at home, but his wild throw up the third base line beaned the batboy. Herndon was awarded third base; Vail, for his part, received two errors and a bad conscience.

COMMENT

Batboy danger calls to mind Game 5 of the 2002 World Series, when a triple by Kenny Lofton scored J.T. Snow and endangered the life of Darren Baker, the three-year-old son of Giants manager Dusty. As Lofton's blast stirred frenzy around the diamond, the diminutive bat boy wandered to home plate to retrieve Lofton's bat. J.T. Snow earned one of the great saves in baseball history when he scooped Baker up after touching the plate. With David Bell tearing toward the plate behind Snow, little Baker was in big jeopardy. (In a game in 2015, a high foul conked the A's ball boy on the head. Fortunately, ball boys wear helmets.)

Vail's two errors on the play where he beaned the batboy were his only errors of the season. He had another statistical anomaly, two year earlier, when he attempted to steal seven bases and was caught each time. (For his career, Vail stole three bases and was caught 17 times, a mind-boggling 15 percent success rate.) But Vail doesn't hold the record for base-stealing futility: Pete Runnells went 0–10 in 1952. Slowpoke? Actually, you probably have to be fast for managers to let you keep trying when you are caught stealing that often. And, in fact, Runnells ran well—he had 64 career triples and 15 in a single season. Stealing requires more than speed.

124: Byrned

On October 4, 2003, in Game 3 of the ALDS between the A's and Red Sox, the A's trailed 1–0 in the sixth inning but threatened with Eric Byrnes at third, Erubiel Durazo at first, one out, and slugger Miguel Tejada at bat. Byrnes tried to score on Tejada's tapper to Derek Lowe, and appeared to succeed when Lowe's throw got away from catcher Jason Varitek. Varitek, however, blocked the plate and sent Byrnes sprawling. As Varitek raced back to the screen to retrieve the ball, Byrnes, angry at the way Varitek blocked the plate, gave him a shove, then did some woofing as he hobbled towards the A's dugout. But he never bothered to touch the plate, and Varitek tagged him out thirty feet from the dish.

COMMENT

Twelve days later, the Red Sox lost in dramatic fashion to the Yankees in Game 7 of the ALCS, Exhibit B (behind only the 1986 World Series) of their 86-year curse that ended the next year. Few remember how lucky the Sox were just to make it to the 2003 ALCS. In the ALDS, they dropped the first two games to the A's, and thus faced three elimination games. They won those games 3–1, 5–4, and 4–3, with the Game 3 win coming in extra innings. That game, and therefore the series, might have been over before then if not for Byrnes' base-running blunder.

Byrnes was also out at the plate on a more bizarre play that makes our top 25. He was an improbable candidate for disaster on the bases. In his career, Byrnes stole 129 bases and was caught only 23 times—a spectacular 85 percent clip. And, off the diamond, he used his impressive speed, playing "speed golf," to set the Guinness Book of World Records mark of 420 holes of golf in a day.

123: Strange Odor

On October 14, 2015, Game 5 of the ALDS, the Rangers and Blue Jays were tied 2–2 in the seventh inning. With the Rangers' Rougned Odor on third, catcher Russell Martin's toss to the mound hit the bat of Shin-soo Choo and rolled down the third base line while Odor hustled in for what proved to be the game-winning run. The play so confounded home-plate umpire, Dale Scott, that he mysteriously sent Odor back to third. But after Rangers manager Jeff Banister convinced him to re-think matters, Scott huddled with the other umpires and reversed himself, allowing the run to count.

COMMENT

This play led to a long, hilarious article by Joe Posnanski, actually a dialogue between him and Michael Schnur, about the entire seventh inning of Game 5. Posnanski said the following about the play in question:

> [I]n freaking baseball, a 19th century game.... Russell Martin in 2015 does something that left me feeling a word I've never once used before because it never quite fit: gobsmacked.... Shin-Soo Choo is standing in the box.... Martin then casually throws the ball back to the pitcher ... only it HITS THE BAT of Shin-Soo Choo and rolls away. Rougned Odor races home. Gobsmacked. Because: NOBODY HAS EVER SEEN THIS BEFORE.[14]

Quipsters might say that, in hitting Choo's bat, Martin was simply throwing to contact—and, as catchers go, he was a good pitcher. In a game in 2019, Martin pitched a 1–2–3 inning, the first field player to do so in almost 60 years. (He needed just ten pitches, including eight strikes.) Later in the season, he became the first position player to pitch in a shutout in more than 100 years. Martin actually closed the Dodgers' 9–0 victory, allowing just one base runner. On the season, he pitched in four games, hurling scoreless innings in each and allowing just two base runners total. He walked zero, struck out two, and faced only one batter over the minimum. Martin, who had not pitched since he was a kid, reached 90 mph on his fastball and threw the occasional off-speed pitch.

122: Team Effort

This is one of the very few plays on the 150 Most Bizarre where I can't supply the details (and it would likely rank higher if we knew them), but the *New York Times* account suffices to establish that the play belongs. On May 16, 1913, the A's defeated the Indians 8–5 with the help of a rally-killing triple-play. Here is how the newspaper of record put it, with characteristic sobriety: "In the seventh Cleveland filled the bases with none out, but all the runners were caught off base by a triple-play in which most of the Philadelphia team participated."[15] The box score does list the six Athletic players involved, including the left fielder, Rube Oldring, so a long run-down must have been involved.

COMMENT

As long as we're staring at a 1913 box score, we might as well note a few other things. First, they had colorful names and nicknames back then. Boardwalk Brown started for the A's, relieved by Chief Bender. The losing pitcher was Vean Gregg, and position players included Stuffy McInnis, Home Run Baker, Ivy Olson, Shoeless Joe Jackson, and Nemo Leibold. Vean Gregg's nickname was derived from his God-given name, which is none too shabby either: Sylveanus Augustus.

Second, the game lasted two hours on the nose, despite the teams combining for 27 hits and 13 runs. That is not the only thing that was different back in those days: The box score also names the *two* umpires. So it was, until a third umpire was added for regular season games in 1933 and a fourth in 1952. Speaking of ways the game has changed, one of the many Philadelphia players to participate in the triple-play was Frank "Home Run" Baker, who earned the nickname by leading the American League in home runs in four consecutive seasons (1911–14). But Baker never hit more than 12 home runs in a season, and hit just 93 total in his 13-year career.

Everyone associates the term "Murderer's Row" with the Ruth-Gehrig Yankee juggernauts from roughly 1925–35, especially 1927. In fact, the term was coined in 1918 (believe it or not by Robert Ripley, the cartoonist who created Ripley's Believe it or Not), before Ruth and Gehrig even joined the team.[16] It was used to describe a Yankees lineup featuring Baker, Wally Pip, Roger Peckinpaugh, Frank Gilhooley, Del Pratt, and Ping Bodie. The team hit a total of 20 home runs, 40 fewer than Ruth alone slugged in 1927, and 27 fewer than Gehrig.

121: 9–2–6–3–2 If You're Scoring

On April 18, 1992, with Dave Gallagher on second and Willie Randolph on first for the Mets in the sixth inning, Mackey Sasser singled to right. The Expos' Larry Walker charged the ball and threw home. Catcher Darren Fletcher tagged Gallagher out at home and then threw to shortstop Tom Foley to try and nab Sasser racing to second. As Sasser retreated into a rundown, Foley threw the ball to first baseman Tim Wallach, at which point Randolph broke for home. Wallach's throw beat him, and Fletcher tagged out Randolph to complete his personal double-play at the plate. (The Expos won the game 8–6, meaning by the margin of Fletcher's putouts on that one play.)

COMMENT

Sasser, whose base hit set this play in motion, experienced a bizarre affliction. Baseball fans know about "Steve Blass Disease," named after the Pirates' star who suddenly lost all semblance of control. In 1973, following a season in which he excelled, Blass walked 84 batters and hit 12 in 88 innings. Other pitchers, such as the heralded Rick Ankiel, caught the disease, as did two second basemen, Steve Sax and Chuck Knoblauch, who found themselves unable to make a simple throw to first. Sax committed 30 errors in 1983, and Knoblauch 26 in 1999, in each case mostly throwing errors. Mackey Sasser may be the only catcher ever afflicted with a version of this disease. In 1990, he developed a severe case of what golfers call the "yips," finding himself unable to throw the ball back to the pitcher without multiple clutches.

In Sasser's case, the affliction was triggered by a specific event: a collision at home plate. That said, there was no diagnosable physical cause of the syndrome. Unlike the "normal" case of Steve Blass Disease (sometimes referred to as Steve Sax Syndrome when it befalls infielders), it did not affect Sasser's performance. He had no difficulty throwing to second and third on attempted steals, or to any base on a batted ball near the plate.

That said, on August 1, 1992, Sasser made a throw that produced a uniquely bad outcome. With the Cubs leading the Mets 5–1 in the eighth, the Mets sensed that Sammy Sosa would attempt to steal second. They pitched out, and had Sosa easily, but Sasser's throw sailed into center field. Such overthrows usually result in an advance of one base at most, but the Mets' centerfielder, Vince Coleman, was oddly positioned and not alert. Sosa scored easily. Six years later, Sosa almost made baseball history by slamming 66 home runs. On this play, he *did* make baseball history—scoring from first while stealing on a pitch-out.

You may wonder why the Mets expected Sosa to run with a four-run lead in the eighth inning. Long before he became known as a slugger, Sosa was a speed demon who stole thirty bases or more in three separate seasons. As for Sasser, his problems carried over to his post-career job as head coach of a community college baseball team: The yips prevented him from pitching batting practice. Eventually, however, psychotherapy helped him solve the problem.

120: Collins Goes Batty

On June 1, 2017, in the fourth inning of the Brewers–Mets game, with the bases loaded and one out the Brewers' Eric Sogard lofted a high pop-up near the Brewers' dugout. The batboy did what batboys are supposed to do in such circumstances: He grabbed his metal stool and tried to scramble away from the third baseman, Wilmer Flores, who raced over to try to catch the ball. But the bat boy failed to stay out of trouble, brushing up against Flores and causing him to miss the ball. The home plate umpire called Sogard out—batboy interference! But after huddling with his crew, he reversed the call. Mets manager Terry Collins was so incensed that he got himself ejected.

COMMENT

The Mets ended up grateful to the bat boy: Given a second chance. Sogard grounded into an inning-ending double-play. As for reversing the interference call, the umpires got that right. As we have seen, Rule 6.01(d) of the official MLB rule book states that the ball remains live when unintentionally interfered with by ballpark personnel. More specifically:

> The question of intentional or unintentional interference shall be decided on the basis of the person's action. For example: a bat boy, ball attendant, policeman, etc., who tries to avoid being touched by a thrown or batted ball but still is touched by the ball would be involved in unintentional interference. If, however, he kicks the ball or picks it up or pushes it, that is considered intentional interference, regardless of what his thought may have been.

Here, the bat boy tried to avoid the ball and did not touch it. Unintentional interference does not result in an out.

We can't know for sure what Collins said to the umpires, but we have some idea thanks to a leaked recording from a 2016 game in which Collins protested after his ace, Noah Syndergaard, was ejected for throwing at a batter. In the videotape, which went viral, Collins charges out and begins by asking, "Are you fucking kidding me?" He gets progressively less polite after that.

119: Tricky Fingers

On October 18, 1972, in the eighth inning of Game 3 of the World Series, the Reds threatened to extend their 1–0 lead. They had runners on first and third with one out, and the fearsome Johnny Bench at the plate. Oakland A's manager Dick Williams brought in his ace reliever, Rollie Fingers, to face Bench. With Bench at bat, Bobby Tolan stole second base, thus opening up first. With a full count on Bench, Williams decided to intentionally walk him. A's catcher Gene Tenace stood up and stuck out his right arm to signal for the free pass, but just as Fingers went into his delivery, Tenace returned to his crouch behind the plate and Fingers delivered strike three down the middle as a stunned Bench watched.

COMMENT

Catcher Tony Pena pulled the same play in both 1996 and 1997 (victimizing Jon Olerud and Brian Johnson, respectively), but we reward originality here. Interestingly, the A's lost Game 3 of the World Series despite Tenace's trickery, just as Cleveland lost both games in which Pena pulled off the fake intentional walk. Draw your own conclusions.

In the department of trickery not succeeding, baseball writers Daniel Okrent and Steve Wulf describe the time Dodgers reliever Clyde King was brought in a game in a hurry and promptly loaded the bases. Trying to buy time for King to throw warm-up pitches, Dodgers manager Charlie Dressen had shortstop Pee Wee Reese fake an eye problem. When Reese did exactly that, teammates Jackie Robinson and Billy Cox came over to assist Reese in trying to get the imaginary something out of his eye. But instead of using the occasions to throw some pitches, the unsuspecting King left the mound to join in the effort to help Reese.[17]

118: Indians Go Ker-Plunk

On May 28, 1993, the Twins and Indians were tied 6–6 in the bottom of the ninth. With runners on second and third and nobody out, Cleveland decided to intentionally walk Kirby Puckett. However, Eric Plunk's first pitch sailed past catcher Lance Parrish for a passed ball, enabling Chuck Knoblauch to cross the plate for the botched intentional walk walk-off win.

COMMENT

Plunk is a great name for a pitcher, though not the equal of Grant Balfour. While you can find numerous lists of baseball's great names, less attention has been paid to the best *collections* of names on a Theme Team. For example, the 1983 Kansas City Royals were a colorful bunch, with Vida Blue, Bud Black, Frank White and, for good measure, Darryl Motley. The New York Mets of the 1980s were the ice cream team, with Strawberry (Darryl), Cone (David), and Howard Johnson. The Phillies of the early 1960s had Bobby Wine and John Boozer. And, for those who like a snack with their alcohol, they also had Cookie Rojas and coach Peanuts Lowrey.

117: Intentional Disaster

On June 22, 2006, the Orioles and Marlins were deadlocked in the tenth inning. With Hanley Ramirez on second and one out, and Miguel Cabrera at bat, the Orioles made the obvious decision to issue an intentional pass. (That year Cabrera hit .339 and drove in 114 runs. On deck stood the unimposing Cody Ross.) The catcher, Ramon Hernandez, signaled for the intentional walk, and stepped way wide of the box to receive the first pitch, but Todd Williams' offering was too close to the plate. The alert Cabrera stroked it into center for a base hit that put the Marlins ahead for good.

COMMENT

In 2017, Major League Baseball changed the rule so the manager merely has to signal his intention to walk the batter. Purists objected, insisting that requiring the pitcher to throw the four pitches is not pro forma. They are certainly right that things can go wrong.

(Ask Cabrera.) Or can go better than expected for the defense. (Ask Johnny Bench, John Olerud, and Brian Johnson who, as we have seen, all struck out on apparent intentional walks.) That said, eliminating the rule saved a little time in an era where baseball games have become interminable.

After the new intentional walk rule was implemented, sportswriter Joe Posnanski raised an interesting question: How would it affect Jon Lester?[18] Because he does not feel capable of lobbing the ball (hence refuses to throw to first to hold a runner), Lester almost never issued an intentional pass. Through 2016, he had just four in his career. For a basis of comparison, consider that James Shields and Adam Wainwright, who both began their careers in 2006 along with Lester, issued 22 and 36 intentional walks respectively. Would the new rule unleash Lester to use the IW from time to time like everyone else? Yes, at first. In 2017, the first year with the new rule, he issued three intentional walks. That's a normal number for a starting pitcher (and three more than usual for Lester). But in 2018 and 2019, he returned to zero. Go figure.

We ought not overlook the bizarreness of Lester's phobia about throwing to first in the first place. This is a guy with excellent control (at least to the plate). For the record, Lester is not the only pitcher who refused to throw to first. Right-hander Sam Jones, who won 102 games during the 1950s and '60s, went five seasons without a single throw to first.[19] Unlike Lester, Jones was not afraid to make the throw. Rather, he believed that the extra throws do more harm than good by taking something out of your arm.

 # 116: Pain in the Neck

The on-deck circle is, by design, located at such an angle from the batter's box that foul balls won't go there. And they don't. But what about broken bats? Isn't the on-deck circle a bit close for comfort? Well, it was never a problem ... until September 6, 1976. On that date, in the seventh inning the Dodgers' Steve Yeager kneeled in the on-base circle minding his business while teammate Bill Russell batted. Russell's broken bat foul ball got Yeager's attention because fragments of the bat lodged in Yeager's throat, perforating his esophagus. Nine shards of wood were surgically removed from his throat.

Comment

The Dodgers won the game 4–1, in a showdown between two pitchers who won 20 games that season: Don Sutton and Randy Jones. Both went the distance, though Jones managed to strike out zero. (On the season, Jones struck out just 93 batters in 315 innings—and won the Cy Young.) If that sounds impressive, consider that, in 1927, a Red Sox pitcher named Ted Wingfield pitched 66 consecutive innings without a strikeout. On the season, he struck out one batter in 74 innings. The sole victim must have been a wild hacker, right? No, it was Max "Camera Eye" Bishop, an impressive contact hitter. (That season, Bishop struck out just 28 times in 492 plate appearances.)

Yeager is the cousin of famous test pilot Chuck Yeager and also the answer to a great trivia question: What Jewish catcher has the most career home runs? Try that on most fans, and you'll likely get Moe Berg as the answer. Berg managed only six home runs in a 16-year career, but is famous thanks to the biography *The Catcher Was a Spy*.[20] And what other Jewish catchers are there? Actually a bunch, including Harry Chozen, Bob Berman, and Brad Ausmus. However, Chozen played in a single game in the majors and Berman just two. They totaled four at-bats between them. (Berman did not get to the plate. Chozen did not homer.) Ausmus swatted 80 home runs. Yeager belted 102, more than all the other Jewish catchers combined.

But wait a minute, Steve Yeager is Jewish? It is a bit of a trick question, because he wasn't Jewish when he played; he converted long afterwards. Philosophers can debate whether his 102 home runs were by a Jewish catcher. The best trivia questions lead to esoteric arguments.

As for Chozen and Berman, what is it with Jewish catchers who play only one or two games? Catch a whiff of anti-Semitism? It is not impossible in Chozen's case, seeing as his solid 17-year minor-league career included a 49-game hitting streak. That streak was almost interrupted at 33, when Chozen, while in the on-deck circle, was struck in the head by a flying bat and knocked unconscious. He had drawn a walk in his only at-bat in that game, and the Southern League commissioner ruled that the streak remained intact. It is an interesting question whether that was the right ruling. Here is a more vexing question:

What is it with Jewish catchers getting hit by flying bats while in the on-deck circle?

115: Stay in Line, Please

On April 14, 2016, in the third inning against the Brewers, Randall Grichuk homered for the Cardinals, but as he rounded first he galloped past teammate Brandon Moss. (Moss had remained on first hoping to tag up if the ball was caught.) That alone doesn't make this an especially bizarre play because, believe it or not, this has happened quite a few times in baseball history. One "detail" makes this play different: Though Grichuk passed Moss by several steps, and in broad daylight, the umpires and Brewers managed to miss it. Despite the base-running blunder, the home run counted.

COMMENT

Weirdly, just 25 days later, another pair of players pulled this same stunt against the Brewers. This time the Marlins J.R. Realmuto passed Marcel Ozuna, and this time the Brewers spotted the infraction and the two-run home run became a harmless single. As noted, this sort of thing happens surprisingly often. Twice in a single season (1930), Babe Herman was passed on the bases by a teammate who hit what should have been a home run. In each case, Herman stopped to admire the flight of the ball and thus allowed himself to be passed. Despite being reasonably fast (he had 94 career stolen bases), Herman is widely considered the worst base runner in baseball history. Sometimes such reputations are unfair. Once an idea takes hold, it becomes hard to shake. In Herman's case, however, the reputation may be deserved. (See Play # 14.) Certainly it formed early. Numerous contemporary newspaper articles casually referred to him as "the worst base runner in baseball" or "a terrible base runner."

Remarkably, Herman was once thrown out attempting to steal by Gabby Street, the 48-year-old Cardinals manager who came into the game as an emergency substitute—his first game in 19 years. (It was not the most impressive moment in Street's long career. On August 21, 1908, he caught a baseball dropped from the top of the Washington Monument—from a distance of some 555 feet. It did, however, take him thirteen tries.)

Herman was also disastrous defensively, and this is documented. In 1927, he led the National League in errors for a first baseman, with a staggering 21. The Dodgers moved him to the outfield, and in 1928 he led the league in errors for an outfielder. He kept that crown in 1929. His teammate Fresco Thompson remarked that Babe "wore a glove for one reason: because it was a league custom." Or as Herman himself told an interviewer, with delightful understatement, "I wasn't the world's greatest fielder, as a lot of stories will attest."[21] But Herman *was* consistent in the field. In four consecutive seasons (from 1927 to 1930), he had exactly 16 errors. In an even more remarkable display of consistency, in four consecutive seasons (2015–2018), the A's Khris Davis hit .247.

114: Tricky Rice

We have seen occasions where the home-run hitter passed a runner who held up because he thought the ball might be caught. On April 26, 1931, in the third inning Lou Gehrig lost a home run because the base runner thought the ball *was* caught. With Lyn Lary on base, a would-be Gehrig round-tripper reached the seats then bounced back onto the field where it was grabbed mid-air by Senators outfielder Harry Rice. The umpires weren't fooled, but the same cannot be said for Lary. Thinking the third out had been made by Rice's catch, Lary returned to the dugout, crossing paths with Gehrig, who was called out for passing a runner. Lary's blunder deprived Gehrig of winning his only home run title outright. (He shared honors with Babe Ruth, each hitting 46.)

COMMENT

The play cost the Yankees two runs and they lost to the Senators 9–7. Not that it much mattered in the end, since that Yankees team finished 13.5 games behind the Athletics, one of baseball's all-time great teams.

A similar play occurred in 1920. Washington's Frank Ellerbe was on first base with two outs when Patsy Gharrity launched a blast into the leftfield bleachers. However, Ellerbe inexplicably thought that Shoeless Joe Jackson caught the ball. Because it would have been the third out, Ellerbe assumed his shortstop position, while Gharrity, circling the bases, trotted past him. Gharrity was called out, leading to the *New York Times'* clever title in its article about the game the next day: "Gharrity's Homer Retires His Side."[22]

History repeated itself on June 19, 1974. The Giants' Ed Goodson sent the Cardinals' Bake McBride to the wall, where McBride appeared to catch the ball. However, the ball popped out of McBride's glove and over the fence for a home run. Phillies base runner Garry Maddox remained between first and second trying to discern what had happened, while Goodson passed him to negate his own home run. The Giants nevertheless won the game 5–4, defeating Bob Gibson, who managed to allow 14 hits and 17 base runners while still pitching a complete game.

The same thing (more or less) happened yet again on April 16, 2006, when the Angels' Darrell Erstadt leaped at the fence to try and rob Javy Lopez of a home run. Erstadt came down hard and lay on the ground, but with or without the ball? The Orioles' Miguel Tejada, the runner on first, mistakenly thought Erstadt had it, and returned to first—and was passed by Lopez in the process.

Literally dozens of players have been cheated out of home runs for other reasons, including: games rained out, forfeited, or called on account of curfew; the batter missing a base on his ceremonial trot; use of an illegal bat; bad calls declaring the ball foul or finding fan interference or mistakenly claiming the ball never left the park (when it bounced in and out of the seats); players batting out of order; failure to complete the trot after a teammate touched the plate to end the game; or a timeout or balk having been called before the pitch.

One lost home run gave rise to a classic Yogi Berra quote. On April 30, 1965, the Mets' Ron Swoboda slugged what should have been a grand slam in Cincinnati. However, Crosley Field featured a double fence; the concrete wall was topped with a plywood extension to protect the construction crew outside. Balls that hit the concrete were in play; the plywood was a home run. Swoboda's ball hit the plywood and bounced back on to the field. The second base umpire erroneously ruled the ball in play, turning Swoboda's home run into a single. Berra, the Mets' first base coach, argued so strenuously that he was ejected. After the game he fumed that "anyone who can't hear the difference between wood and concrete must be blind."[23]

113: Never Mind, You're Still Out

A similar play that occurred decades after Gehrig and Gharrity lost their homers gets a higher ranking because it involved more elements. On August 7, 2018, with one out in the third inning of a scoreless game between the Braves and Nationals, and Trea Turner on first, Juan Soto's blast sent centerfielder Ender Inciarte to the fence in left-center. Inciarte made a leaping try and seemed to bat the ball in the air. Left fielder Adam Duvall swooped in and grabbed the ball before it hit the ground, completing a brilliant tag-team catch. Turner sped back to first. However, replay review revealed that the ball hit the wall after Inciarte got his glove on it, negating Duvall's catch. The Nats were the ones who asked for review, but winning it did them no good: Soto was nevertheless out because he passed Turner before the non-catch. Actually it is misleading to say Soto passed Turner. After they both deemed the ball caught, Soto (who was between first and second) started walking back to the dugout whereas Turner (who had made it to second) sprinted back to first. Turner whizzed past Soto, but going in the wrong direction, which means Soto, the trail runner, was the one ruled out for doing the passing. Got it?

COMMENT

In the previous season, 2017, Turner and Inciarte accomplished extraordinary feats: Turner stole four bases in a game (a club record) twice in less than two weeks while Inciarte had five-hit games twice in less than two weeks. Turner and Soto were also both involved in bizarre situations on account of baseball quirks with respect to timing. Soto debuted in the majors on May 20, 2018, but hit his first home run five days earlier on May 15. Say what? The May 15 game was suspended with the score tied. Soto homered when the game was resumed on June 18. The date of the game technically remains May 15. Turner, for his part, was traded by the Padres to the Nationals on December 19, 2014, though he was officially designated a "player to be named later" because a player cannot be traded until a year after he is drafted. In reality, he was a player "named sooner but traded later." He spent April through mid–June of 2015 with the Padres' organization, waiting to become a Nat on June 16. The Padres kept Turner in the minors (with no motivation to foster his development), perhaps in part to prevent the weirdness of him playing for a team he knew he would leave. Imagine if Turner got in a game for the Padres against the Nats. That would be a rare case of a player with a conflict of interest.

112: Honest Base-Running

On April 13, 2019, with two outs in the top of the first inning, the Angels' Justin Bour lined a base hit into the right-field corner. He took a wide turn around first, then decided to settle for a single. As the Cubs' right fielder, Ben Zobrist, threw behind him, Bour dove back to first. Zobrist's throw hit Bour's foot and careened away. The extremely slow Bour got up and chugged into second but the throw by the Cubs' catcher, Wilson Contreras, to shortstop Javier Baez, arrived well before Bour. However, Baez, who is known for his amazingly dexterous tags, was a little too casual with this one. He picked up the tag before touching Bour. That, at any rate, is what umpire Marty Foster saw. He called Bour safe. But Bour voluntarily left the bag and headed for the dugout. Baez tracked him down between first and second and tagged him out.

Comment

There are two possibilities. Most likely, Bour didn't hear Foster call him safe. Alternatively, he simply disagreed with the call and expected replay review to confirm his view and decided to save everyone time. I'm not sure which would be weirder: Even if you know you're out, you're not supposed to assume that the umpire has gotten it right or that the replays will be clear enough to overturn him.

Bour made another base-running blunder just six days later, and this one gives rise to a question that all little-leaguers should have to answer: Why does the infield rule apply only when there are runners on both first and second? The purpose of the rule is to prevent infielders from purposely missing a fly so they can get a double-play. But there is no risk of that if there is only one runner forced, because as long as the batter runs to first (and there is no good reason not to), there is no chance of a double-play. *As long as the runner runs to first.* On April 19, against the Mariners, with a runner on first Bour lofted a routine pop-up, and started walking back to the dugout in disgust. Third baseman Ryon Healy let the ball bounce, picked it up on a hop, and tossed it to Tim Beckham at second for the force. Beckham lobbed it to first (with Bour nowhere in sight) for the double play. Bour's blunder ended the Angels' eighth inning, keeping the score tied. The Mariners scored two in the ninth to win 5–3.

#111: *Quadruple Steal*

We have seen countless double steals, and even triple steals, but how about a double double steal? Or is that a quadruple steal? On August 1, 1985, with Vince Coleman on second and Willie McGee on first in the top of the first inning, the Cardinals attempted a double steal. Coleman made it safely to third but over-slid the bag. He would have been tagged out by Cubs third baseman Ron Cey, so he sprinted home—why not? The Cubs had him in a rundown, but somehow left home plate uncovered, allowing Coleman to score. That happens—in little league, anyway. Meanwhile, while the Cubs were preoccupied with Coleman, McGee made it all the way to third. Both Coleman and McGee were credited with two steals on the play.

COMMENT

Coleman, a base-stealer for the ages, stole *more than one hundred bases* in each of his first three years in the majors. He was a sensational all-around athlete who played college football and gave the NFL serious consideration. It is easy to imagine the speedy Coleman as a running back or wide receiver or perhaps defensive back, right? Actually, he was a field goal kicker and punter. Go figure.

Some observers thought Coleman was the fastest player in baseball history. Other candidates include Tim Raines, Mickey Mantle, Deion Sanders, Bo Jackson, and Cool Papa Bell of the Negro leagues. (Of Cool Papa it was often said that he could turn off the lights and get under covers before it was dark.) The case can be made that it must be someone playing today, perhaps Billy Hamilton, seeing as athletes seem to get faster and faster—just look at how most Olympic track records are reasonably short-lived. But it is not impossible that the fastest player of all time was born in the nineteenth century.

Consider the credentials of Hans Lobert, a solid third baseman for three National League teams from 1903 to 1917. Lobert won a footrace against the legendary Jim Thorpe, an Olympic gold medalist in track. (To be sure, Thorpe won gold in the pentathlon and decathlon, not in sprints.) Perhaps more impressively, Lobert held a *horse* to a virtual tie in a race around the bases. Lobert always insisted that he led the horse easily mid-way through the race, but as he tore between second and third, the horse, coming from the opposite direction, almost bowled him over and knocked him off balance, slowing his pace. In any event, the legendary umpire Bill Klem gave the horse the nod by a nose.

It is difficult to compare Lobert on the bases with other speed-sters. He stole 40 or more bases four times but before 1920 the "caught stealing" statistic was kept only unofficially and somewhat haphaz-ardly. Baseball Reference lists no figure for Lobert's caught steal-ing until 1913, omits it in 1914, and resumes it in 1915, his last season. In 1913 and 1915, Lobert stole a combined 55 bases and was caught 36 times. Nothing special, but he was at the end of his career. In his prime, he held a horse to a draw!

Given the nature of progress in all sports, the obvious fact that ath-letes are bigger and stronger and train better, it may seem absurd to suggest that any early twentieth-century player could possibly match Billy Hamilton stride for stride. But we need to heed the lesson of sci-entist and baseball fan Steven Jay Gould that, in certain activities, humans approach the limits of excellence—there is just not much room for improvement. It is doubtful that in 100 years anyone will hit the ball much further than Mickey Mantle or throw much harder than Walter Johnson. And the fastest baseball player in the nineteenth century may have approached the human limit when it comes to straightaway speed.

That said, in all likelihood the fastest baseball player ever was nei-ther Lobert nor Hamilton nor any of the other speedsters mentioned above. It was Herb Washington, the track star whom Charles Finley used as a pinch-runner in the 1970s. Washington, the ultimate spe-cialist, entered 105 games but never came to bat or played in the field. Including the post-season, he stole 31 bases in 50 attempts, a decid-edly mediocre 62 percent. Conclusive proof, if any were needed, that there is much more to base stealing than speed.

110: Catcher's Mask Loses Game

On August 12, 1995, the Pirates and Dodgers were hooked up in a strange game with a delightful score: 10–10 after ten innings. In the bottom of the eleventh, the Dodgers threatened to push across the winning run, as Roberto Kelly reached third with one out. With Mitch Webster at bat, Jeff McCurry's 1–0 pitch bounced in the dirt. The Pirates catcher, Angelo Encarnación (who entered the game that inning), blocked the ball, then scooped it up with his gloved left hand. So far so good. However, the ball bounced out of the glove and into his mask which he was holding with his right hand. Ballgame over.

As soon as Encarnación handled the ball with his mask, an alert Tommy Lasorda charged out of the dugout to inform the umpires that Encarnación violated a little-known rule prohibiting a player from handling a ball with a uniform part. Kelly was awarded home, and the Dodgers enjoyed an 11–10 "walk-off violation" victory.

COMMENT

The rule in question is 7.05(d): "Each runner including the batter-runner may, without liability to be put out, advance ... two bases, if a fielder deliberately touches a thrown ball with his cap, mask or any part of his uniform detached from its proper place on his person. The ball is in play."

Did Tommy Lasorda have the rulebook memorized? No. But it just so happens that the same rule had cost the Dodgers a run just three years earlier, when their catcher, Mike Scioscia, suffered the same rare fate as Encarnación. The Dodgers lost that game to the Padres 4–3. Those two occasions, each involving the Dodgers, each accounting for the winning run, just three years apart, were perhaps the only times the rule had been invoked in baseball history.

A similar ruling would involve the Dodgers a third time 21 years later, this time victimizing them. On July 31, 2016, Ross Stripling's pitch bounced in the dirt, popped up and struck catcher Yasmani Grandal in the neck, then rolled inside the catcher's chest protector. When Grandal managed to extract the ball, he received the bad news from home plate umpire Todd Tichenor: Catcher's interference, allowing the runner on third to score. Fortunately for the Dodgers, Grandal clubbed two three-run home runs in the game, leading them to a 14–3 win.

 # 109: Harri Houdini

On June 27, 2014, in the top of the tenth inning against the Mets, Pittsburgh's Josh Harrison was on second base when Gregory Polanco topped a ball to the mound that was snagged by pitcher Jenrry (no typo) Mejia. Harrison broke for third, but got caught in a rundown. Second baseman Ruben Tejada chased Harrison toward third and tossed the ball to third baseman Ike Davis, who chased Harrison back toward second. When Davis sought to make the tag, however, Harrison did a Houdini act. He somehow escaped untagged, and now headed for third with Davis still in pursuit. Davis threw to Tejada, who moved in for the tag, but Harrison did *another* Houdini act to elude him. He finally dove head-first into third safely. Two additional details emerge from multiple viewings of this play. First, Harrison changed direction *six* times. Second, in the middle of the play, Harrison threw his helmet to the ground. The bouncing helmet only added to the chaos, and surely didn't help the infielders.

Lest you think the play a fluke, exactly one month later, on July 27, Harrison did pretty much the same thing against the Rockies. This time he stole second on a pitchout, but his slide took him past the bag. No worries, he just headed for third. Another rundown, another Houdini act, again resulting in Harrison safe at third, this time leaving catcher Wilin Rosario on his butt in between second and third with the ball lying on the ground nearby.

Comment

In the June 27 game, after Harrison did all that work to reach third, he was stranded. No problem. In the next inning he doubled home Cliff Barnes to give the Pirates a walk-off win.

After the July 27 game, Harrison, who also had four hits and a game-winning home run on the afternoon, explained his derring-do: "It's easy for me to try to make something happen as opposed to trying to reach back to second because he was right there. And something happened. More and more I got into it, I was able to kind of set up some moves to where I might be able to be safe."[24]

"Set up some moves?" As if Harrison practices defeating rundowns! Who knows, maybe he does. But his two base-running escapades one month apart looked to the naked eye like spectacular improvisation.

Many plays missed making the 150 Most Bizarre Plays because they were similar to, but not quite as bizarre as, one or more plays on the list. In this case, Harrison's rundowns knocked out some strong competitors, particularly a play resulting in a run and credit for a steal of home for Alcides Escobar. It is pretty much the only way players steal home these days, on a double steal, with Escobar breaking for the plate after Alex Gordon was caught in a rundown between first and second. The Indians handled things just right, keeping an eye on Escobar throughout and abandoning Gordon as soon as Escobar got too far off the bag. The throw from Nick Swisher to third trapped Escobar, now the subject of a new rundown. However, he eventually dodged a lunging Yan Gomes, the catcher, and scored. That's 2–6–3–4–3–5–2. A lot of work by the defense for zero outs.

The most famous botched rundown ended the 1917 World Series. Third baseman Heinie Zimmerman chased the White Sox's Eddie Collins across home plate because none of his Giants teammates were covering home. A similar play makes my Top 5 because it has a much grander ending.

108: Sly Foxx

On October 2, 1931, Game 2 of the 1931 World Series, in the ninth inning the Cardinals were trying to protect a two-run lead but the Athletics put Jimmie Foxx on second and Jimmy Dykes on first with two outs and Jimmy Moore at bat. With the count 0–2, Foxx and Dykes attempted a daring double steal. However, Moore swung and missed— strike three, end of game. Except the pitch from Wild Bill Hallahan was in the dirt and bounced before being scooped up by catcher Jimmie Wilson. So Wilson threw to first to complete the strikeout and end the game, right? Nope, he threw to third to try to catch Foxx stealing. With the missed third strike entitling Moore to head for first, the play at third became a force play. Third baseman Jack Flowers compounded the folly by trying to tag Foxx instead of stepping on the base. Foxx was safe, and now the bases were loaded.

COMMENT

Hallahan retired Max Bishop on a pop to first, with a fine running catch by Jim Bottomley sparing Wilson the goat horns.

Note that there were four players named Jimmy or Jimmie involved in the play. As for the one who made a near-historic blunder, catcher Wilson, not everyone considered his throw to third a mistake.

Team captain Frankie Frisch claimed that Wilson made a smart play.[25] Having seen the two runners in motion, he knew that allowing them to steal would put the tying runs in scoring position. Accordingly, he made up his mind to throw while the pitch was on the way. He wasn't planning on catching a bounced strike three.

There are two other footnotes to the play. First, the official scorer charged Wilson with an error for throwing to the wrong base and did not award stolen bases to Foxx and Dykes. And Wilson, the goat on the play (notwithstanding Frisch's generous assessment), became a most improbable World Series hero nine years later in a storybook ending to his long career. In 1938 and '39, Wilson played in just seven games total, and retired after the '39 season. However, in 1940 he joined the Reds mid-season to provide the team another catcher (after backup Willard Hershberger committed suicide, the only major leaguer ever to do so during the season). When all-star backstop Ernie Lombardi suffered an injury late in the season, Wilson saw some action and played well. He started six of the seven games in the 1940 World Series, and batted .353. He then retired for good—a World Series champion.

107: Merkle's Boner

Even the casual fan has heard of "Merkle's Boner," but even devout fans may not know just how strange the play was. On September 23, 1908, in the midst of a pennant race, the Giants and Cubs were tied 1–1 in the bottom of the ninth. The Cubs had runners on first and third and two outs, when Al Bridwell lined a base hit that seemed to win the game. However, instead of running to second base, the runner at first, Fred Merkle, sprinted to the clubhouse past the outfield to avoid the crowd swarming the field. Cubs second baseman Johnny Evers (of Tinkers to Evers to Chance fame) recognized as much, and called for the ball so he could step on second for the inning-ending force play to negate the seeming walk-off win.

Easier said than done. Figuring out what actually happened suffers from the "fog of war" syndrome. On some accounts, Giants great Christy Mathewson saw what was happening and sprinted to the clubhouse to summon Merkle to return to second (but didn't make it in time). The umpires' whereabouts during the ensuing chaos is also subject to various accounts. What we know for sure is that Evers' plan to retrieve the baseball from center-fielder Artie "Solly" Hofman ran amok. Evers' frantic waving and screaming did eventually get Hofman's attention. Hofman danced around the fans in the outfield to retrieve the ball. Exactly what happened next is lost to history, including whether Evers ever retrieved the original ball and stepped on second base with an umpire watching. In any event, the head umpire, Hank O'Day, declared Merkle out at second, preserving the 1–1 tie.

Contemporary newspaper accounts differed on all the details and the participants in the play gave varied accounts over the years. I would like to think that the recollection of Giants outfielder Fred Snodgrass (who is almost as famous for his World Series "muff" as Merkle is for his "boner") is accurate. Snodgrass offered his version in *The Glory of Their Times*, Lawrence Ritter's sensational oral history of baseball's early days. According to Snodgrass, the Cubs' third-base coach, Joe McGinity, saw Evers' plot in action, intercepted Hofman's throw into the infield, and threw the ball into the left-field bleachers.[26] This account has a certain plausibility, because "Iron Man" McGinity was a star pitcher with a great arm. (He was still pitching. Players occasionally doubled as coaches in those days.)

COMMENT

The game went down as a tie because, with the crowd still swarming the field, O'Day called the game on account of darkness. The league upheld the ruling, and the Giants and Cubs ended up with identical records at the conclusion of the regular season. The Cubs won the playoff game, sending them to the World Series and Merkle to infamy. How sorry one should feel for Merkle is an open question. He was 19 at the time, and went on to have a long, successful career, playing in five World Series. But his teams lost all five.

It would seem that Merkle's Boner was a once-in-a-lifetime play, if only because it was so publicized. What base runner in the future would fail to reach the next base in a walk-off situation? Believe it or not, *two* runners did so in a game in 2015. But precisely because there were two of them, it turned out okay. Huh?

In a game against the Reds, the Diamondbacks loaded the bases in the tenth inning, and Chris Owings' drive over the head of Billy Hamilton plated Paul Goldschmidt with what seemed like the game-ending run. However, the runners at first and second, David Peralta and Jake

Lamb, joined in the celebration between home and first rather than advancing to the next base. The Reds retrieved the ball, and raced it over to third base and then second base for what they contended was an inning-ending double-play thanks to a Double Merkle's Boner! (Or, less poetically, a Peralta-Lamb Boner.)

Alas, it turns out, the rulebook apparently prevents the Double Merkle's Boner. The explanation is insanely complicated, not to mention dubious, so I prefer the back-up explanation for the ruling: Apparently a security guard touched the ball in the outfield prior to the Reds returning it to the infield. That interference rendered the play dead at which point allowing the run to score seems a reasonable exercise of umpire's discretion. (While we have seen that play continues during "unintentional interference" by security, this was intentional.)

Another variation on the theme of Merkle's Boner took place on June 8, 1961, in a game between the Red Sox and Angels. The Sox trailed 4–3 in the bottom of the eleventh. After a leadoff walk to Chuck Schilling, Gary Geiger tripled to score Schilling and tie the game. However, mistakenly thinking the game over, an exultant Geiger raced to the clubhouse. Oops. He was declared out, costing the Sox a great opportunity to score and end the game (the second of a twilight doubleheader). Instead, it was called on account of curfew with the score tied.

The year of 1967 was an eventful season for Geiger. On May 27, less than two weeks before his blunder, he dropped a Brooks Robinson fly with the score tied 4–4 and two outs in the bottom of the ninth, handing the Orioles a win. But exactly two months after the base-running blunder, on August 8, Geiger hit an inside-the-park grand slam—one of just three by a Red Sox in Fenway Park history.

 # 106: Dazzy's Dazzling Improvisation

On September 16, 1930, with the Cardinals and Robins in a scoreless game in the sixth inning, the Cards had Sparky Adams on third base and Chick Hafey at bat against Dazzy Vance. With the count 0–2, Adams caught the Robins by surprise and sprinted down the line for an attempted steal of home. He had the base stolen, except Vance improvised brilliantly: He threw at Hafey. The hit batsman meant a dead ball, and the return of Adams to third.

The Plays

COMMENT

With two strikes on the batter, the theft of home seems crazy—the batter has to swing at a strike and risk decapitating the runner. On the other hand, if Adams was sure he could make it, *and* sure that Vance planned a waste pitch with the count 0–2, *and* sure that Hafey could hear him screaming not to swing, it was a brilliant play—negated by Vance's brilliant reaction.

Vance's brilliance paid off insofar as he proceeded to retire the side without the run scoring. However, a run in the tenth broke the scoreless tie for the Cardinals. Both Vance and the Cardinals' Bill Hallahan pitched ten innings, which would be a miracle if it happened today.

Vance's alertness calls to mind the most impactful heads-up play ever—a base-running gem by Mickey Mantle in the ninth inning of Game 7 of the 1960 World Series. Mantle was on first and Gil McDougald on third with one out and the Yankees trailing the Pirates 9–8. Yogi Berra hit a sharp grounder to first, where Rocky Nelson fielded it and stepped on the bag for the second out. Nelson now faced two options for attempting a series-ending double-play: throw home to nail McDougald or throw to second to get Mantle. But Mantle confounded matters by *diving back to first*. (Nelson stepping on the bag eliminated the force on Mantle.) Nelson reached to tag Mantle, but too late, and McDougald scampered home with the tying run—setting up Bill Mazeroski's dramatic walk-off home run for the Pirates.

 # 105: Defensive Indifference

On May 22, 2010, in the fourth inning of a 2–2 game, Nationals centerfielder Nyjer Morgan made a leaping attempt near the wall on a long fly off the bat of Baltimore's Adam Jones, but could not quite make the play. The ball went off his glove, then off the wall, then fell to the ground. Morgan was so disgusted that he fired his glove to the ground, and ignored left fielder Josh Willingham screaming at him to retrieve the ball. Jones raced around the bases. Willingham chased the ball down and the Nationals made the play at the plate reasonably close. Still, the result was an inside-the-park home run assisted by defensive indifference.

COMMENT

According to post-game accounts, Morgan thought the ball had gone over the fence after hitting his glove. Morgan's teammates and manager were forgiving. "My first instinct was to take him out of the ballgame," manager Jim Riggleman said. "Then I realized, you know what, he thinks the ball went over the fence. He thought that he knocked it over the fence, and it's a home run, and he's showing frustration."[27] Riggleman may have felt forgiving because a four-run seventh inning gave the Nats the win. No thanks to Morgan, who also committed a first-sinning error that helped the O's plate a pair.

Morgan had a tough 2010 all around. He hit zero home runs in 577 plate appearances, one fewer than he gifted Adam Jones. In August, he was suspended seven games for throwing a ball at a fan in Philadelphia. Six days later, while that suspension was under appeal, he charged the mound and started a bench-emptying brawl that led to an eight-game suspension. (Maybe not surprising considering that Morgan played semi-professional hockey.) And, for good measure, he led the league in caught stealing with 17.

His manager, Riggleman, also had a tough 2010, and a worse 2011. In 2010, he led the Nats to a dismal record of 69–93. They did better the next year: In fact, in mid–June they won 11 out of 12 games to pass .500 at 38–37. Riggleman apparently thought that was a good time to demand a contract extension. The club's general manager, Mike Rizzo, disagreed, and Riggleman resigned. Proving just how important most managers are, the rest of the way the club went 42–44, almost identical to their performance with Riggleman at the helm.

104: Gonzo Ending

In the fourth inning of the Giants–Padres game on April 21, 2009, Kevin Kouzmanoff's blast off the right-field wall sent two runners scampering home. Because the lead runner, Adrian Gonzalez, held up to see if the ball would be caught, the trail runner, Chase Headley, almost overtook him, and the two Padres arrived at the plate along with the relay throw home. Gonzalez slid wide, evading the tag of catcher Bengie Molina but also missing the plate. Home plate umpire, Jeff Nelson, properly made no call—to that point Gonzalez was neither safe nor out. A split-second later, Headley found the plate blocked and tried leap-frogging Molina. He was unsuccessful, and called out. Now, both Gonzalez and Molina lay sprawled on the ground, Gonzalez's fate unresolved. He dove back toward the plate, while Molina dove to tag him. Gonzalez was safe by a hair. Thus the trail base runner was out at the plate before the lead base runner scored.

COMMENT

As bizarre as this play was, it could have been more so. If Headley had slid in safely under the tag, he presumably would have been declared out for passing Gonzalez. And if Gonzalez had been out at home instead of barely safe, the Giants would have recorded a double-play with both outs coming on tag plays at home plate, one after another. (Believe it or not, that has happened several times. Keep reading.) Molina argued furiously that he had in fact tagged Gonzalez in time for the crazy double-play. It is too bad Headley did not dispute being called out, or we would have had two simultaneous arguments—one from each team—with the umpire. (Think that's never happened? Again, keep reading.)

Apart from his participation in this chaos, Kouzmanoff achieved some distinctions. That 2009 season, he committed just three errors in 309 chances: His .990 fielding percentage remains the best single-season mark by a third baseman in National League history. Three years earlier, as a rookie with the Indians, Kouzmanoff swatted the first pitch he saw in the major leagues for a grand slam, the first player ever to do so. Four years later, Daniel Nava replicated the feat.

 # 103: Split Decision

Believe it or not, almost the exact same play occurred more than a century earlier. On August 9, 1905, in the seventh inning of the Cubs' victory over the Giants, a bases-loaded double by Frank Chance (off the legendary Iron Man Joe McGinty) did not quite clear the bases. While Bob Wicker, the runner from third, of course scored easily, and Jimmy Slagle slid in barely safe for the second run, right behind him Billy Maloney was tagged out by catcher Roger Bresnahan.

COMMENT

This play gets the nod over its virtually identical play in 2009 because it did indeed produce simultaneous arguments. From the next day's *New York Times*: "New York contended that both men were out, while Chicago wanted both men called safe."[28]

Frank Chance, of Tinkers to Evers to Chance fame, had a nice day: 4–4 with two stolen bases. Chance illustrates the fickleness of reputation. Whereas Joe Tinkers and Johnny Evers are undoubtedly overrated as a result of the legendary poem, Chance may be *underrated* for the same reason. At least to the casual fan, Frank Chance is the guy who was lucky enough to play first base with the amazing double-play combination of Tinkers and Evers. In fact, Chance had a lifetime on-base percentage of .396 and twice led the league in stolen bases. Tinkers, Evers, and Chance were jointly inducted into the Hall of Fame in 1946. Chance is the only one who probably would have made it without the poem.

While most fans know the Franklin Pierce Adams' poem ("Baseball's Sad Lexicon") that immortalized the trio, less well known is the Ogden Nash poem, "Lineup for Yesterday," that includes the following lines: "E is for Evers/His jaw in advance/ Never afraid/To Tinker with Chance."

102: Insult Added to Injury

On May 8, 1973, with the Mets leading 3–1 in the seventh inning, the Braves loaded the bases with two outs against Jon Matlack. With the rain falling, and a full count on Marty Perez, the drama built towards a climax no one imagined. Perez slammed the payoff pitch off Matlack's forehead, and the ball detoured into the Mets' dugout—a game-tying ground rule double that never left the infield. As everyone awaited the stretcher to carry Matlack off, the trainer covered him with the rubber tarp that was brought out to cover the field as the rain picked up.

COMMENT

Matlack suffered a fractured skull but missed only two starts. This was before the era of concussion protocols, and macho "achievements" like Matlack's were not all that uncommon. On Opening Day in 1936, with President Franklin D. Roosevelt in attendance, pitcher Bobo Newsom was struck in the face by a throw to first from his third baseman. After recovering, he pitched a four-hit shutout against the mighty Yankees. Then he got his jaw wired: It had been broken in two places.

Newsom had a quirky personality and quirky career. He lost 20 games three times, and sported a losing record overall—remarkable for a guy who lasted 24 years. In 1934, he went 16–20, with an ERA of 4.01. Four years later, he turned it around and went 20–16, with the decidedly worse ERA of 5.08. In the words often attributed to another colorful pitcher, Lefty Gomez, you're better off lucky than good. For the record, that same Lefty Gomez was the opposing pitcher on that 1936 Opening Day. He matched Newsom goose egg for goose egg until the bottom of the ninth when Carl Reynolds doubled home Cecil Travis with the winning run.

Speaking of luck, on account of poor timing—this thing called World War II—Travis had a superb career derailed. In his first eight years, he batted over .300 seven times. In 1941, the year Joe DiMaggio hit in 56 straight games, Travis out-hit Joe D (.359 to .357). However, Travis missed the next three years to military service. He fought as an infantryman in the Battle of the Bulge, suffering severe frostbite that required surgery. He received a Bronze Star. But when he returned to baseball, though still only 31, he was pretty much through.

Jon Matlack also understood the importance of luck. Over his 13-year career, he lost one more game than he won (125–126) despite a stellar ERA of 3.18. And that ERA was inflated by Matlack's end-of-career struggles with the Rangers. With the Mets, he had ERAs of 2.32, 2.41, and 2.27. In those three seasons, he won barely more than he lost. In 2020, the Mets inducted him into their Hall of Fame. Had he pitched for a team with more offense, he just might have found himself in *the* Hall of Fame. The die was cast in Matlack's debut, on July 11, 1971. He stymied Cincinnati's Big Red Machine, scattering six hits in seven innings, walking none, and yielding just one run. He left with a 2–1 lead, but Tom Seaver blew the save, allowing a three-run homer to Tony Perez. Wait, Tom Seaver in relief? That season, Seaver pitched in 36 games, winning 20, and that was his sole outing in relief. It was the last game before the All-Star game, and back then managers treated such games as all-hands-on-deck.

101: He Spiked the Baseball!

Poor Corey Kluber was very good but very unlucky on July 24, 2014. The Indians' ace lost a perfect game on a groundball single in the seventh inning, but the game remained scoreless. In the eighth, the Royals' Mike Moustakas lofted a high fly down the left field line. Ryan Raburn made a long run and attempted a backhanded diving catch, but the ball went off his glove, bounced around his arm, then hit the ground and rolled to the wall in foul territory. Moustakas cruised into second. Raburn ran down the ball and made a throw for the ages, basically imitating a football player celebrating a touchdown with an end-zone spike. As the ball rolled harmlessly to center field, Moustakas sprinted around the bases courtesy of a throw so bad that few little leaguers would make it.

COMMENT

It makes the play no less incredible, but it turns out there was an explanation for Raburn's disastrous throw. Moustakas' high fly sent the Indians scrambling, with the third baseman Lonnie Chisenhall heading to the outfield and others belatedly trying to cover third. When Raburn cocked to throw the ball to third, he saw no one there, and tried to hold up his throw. On Sports Illustrated's website, Jon Tayler discussed the play uncharitably: "Raburn's blunder will go down in the books as a double and an error, but really, how else do you mark that other than 'outfielder-assisted inside-the-park home run?' Raburn would have been better off firing the ball over the left field wall once he picked it up."[29]

The game remained 1–0 when the Indians came to bat for their last chance in the ninth. A leadoff walk to Carlos Santana brought up Raburn with a chance for redemption. But Tribe manager Terry Francona, clearly not a romantic, sent up a pinch-hitter. The Indians tied the game and won it in 14 innings. Kluber, though deprived of the shutout and the win, went on to win the Cy Young that season.

100: Out of Left Field

This play is similar to the previous play, but was a bit more involved and occurred during one of the wackiest post-season games in baseball history. On October 11, 1980, in Game 4 of the 1980 NLCS between the Astros and Phillies, with one out in the bottom of the fourth inning of a scoreless game, the Astros had Enos Cabell on third, Gary Woods at first, and Art Howe at bat against Steve Carlton. Howe lofted a fly to fairly deep left that Lonnie Smith caught as both runners tagged up. But when Smith went to throw the ball, it fell out of his hand, rolled off his shoulder, hit the ground, and sped away on the turf toward the infield. Cabell scored easily, Smith chased after the ball, and Woods raced around second and kept going to third. Smith finally caught up to the ball and threw to third, but off-line. Mike Schmidt ranged way off the bag to catch the throw, then made a valiant effort to get Smith with a diving tag. He was too late ... except the umpire called Smith out. The Astros protested mightily, but not all was lost: Cabell's run did count, as he crossed the plate prior to the third out.

COMMENT

This is the single game to feature two plays in the 150 Most Bizarre Plays. The other play, much higher on this list, involved the entire umpiring crew and, for good measure, the National League president, and left both teams bitterly unhappy. (You won't get there for a while. That play is a doozy.) Since one of these plays was in the top of the fourth inning, and the other the bottom, this inning lays a strong claim to being the most bizarre in baseball history.

Another post-season game produced arguably the most bizarre *half-inning* in baseball history. In the bottom of the third of the 2018 NLCS between the Dodgers and Brewers, Clayton Kershaw came out to pitch with a 1–0 lead. Pitcher Brandon Woodruff started things in style for the Brewers with a 400-foot home run. A seemingly rattled Kershaw gave up a single to Lorenzo Cain and walked Christian Yelich. With one out, a passed ball through the legs of Yasmani Grandal moved the runners to second and third. Jesus Aguilar hit a screamer to right, but David Freeze made a spectacular diving catch. However, Aquilar's bat nicked Grandal's glove (Aguilar later said he had no idea), and the catcher's interference negated the great catch and loaded the bases. Hernan Perez hit a sacrifice fly, and Grandal somehow fanned on Cody Bellinger's decent throw home, allowing another run to score. Three runs on two hits, one walk and a trifecta by Grandal—a passed ball, interference, and an error. (The only other catcher to manage that feat in a single post-season inning was Matt Wieters, one year earlier to the day, in the 2017 NLDS Game 5.) By the time it was over, everyone had forgotten that the inning began with a mortar shot by a pitcher off Clayton Kershaw. It wasn't a complete fluke. Woodruff can hit. That regular season, he batted .250 with a home run.

99: Tragedy and Farce: Six Twin Killings at Home

Remember Play # 104, featuring Bengie Molina trying to tag two players at the same time? I noted that, had Molina been a little luckier, "the Giants would have recorded a double-play with both outs coming on tag plays at home plate!" That's actually happened ... *six times*! The first was April 19, 1923, in the fifth inning of a Braves–Giants game. With Billy Southworth on second and Tony Boeckel on first, Bill Bagwell lofted a ball to deep right. Southworth held the bag to tag, so when the ball fell safely, Boeckel was on his heels. They both raced around the bases and arrived at the plate at virtually the same time. Meanwhile right fielder Ross Youngs hit the cutoff man, Frankie Frisch, whose relay to catcher Frank Snyder caught both runners. In the next day's *Boston Globe*, National League president John A. Heydler was quoted as saying that, so far as he knew, the play was unique in baseball history.[30] It would not remain that way.

Oddly, in three of the remaining double-plays at home, it was the Yankees who managed to have a pair of players tagged out by one catcher on one throw. The first such occasion was April 29, 1933, when the Bombers hosted the Washington Senators. In the bottom of the ninth, trailing 6–3, the Yankees had Lou Gehrig on second and Dixie Walker on first. When Tony Lazzeri doubled to right-center, the speedy Walker almost overtook Gehrig as they both arrived at the plate. Outfielder Goose Goslin threw to Joe Cronin whose relay to catcher Luke Sewell was in time for Sewell to tag out Gehrig and Walker in quick succession.

Karl Marx famously said that history repeats itself, the first time as tragedy and the second as farce. In this case, the two-out-at-the-plate repeated itself as both tragedy and farce on August 28, 1979. The Brewers batting against the Royals in the top of the 8th inning had

Cecil Cooper on second base and Gorman Thomas on first. On Ben Oglivie's double, the relays from Amos Otis to Frank White to catcher Darrell Porter nailed both Cooper and Thomas at the plate.

The next improbable reoccurrence was just six years later. On August 2, 1985, the Yankees were again the victims. They were tied 3–3 with the White Sox in the seventh inning at Yankee Stadium. With Bobby Meacham on second base and Dale Berra on first, Rickey Henderson drove the ball over the head of center-fielder Ozzie Guillen. Meacham stumbled, so Berra ended up close behind, and decided to follow his teammate all the way home. Guillen hit the cut-off man, Luis Salazar, who threw to Carlton Fisk, who tagged out Meacham and Berra in quick succession.

The Yankees were again victimized on September 28, 2000, against the Devil Rays in Tampa Bay. In the top of the second, with Jose Canseco on second, Tino Martinez drove a base hit to deep center field and thoughts raced through his head of an inside-the-park home run. However, for that to happen, Canseco had to score first. Catcher Mike DiFelice tagged Canseco out and then tagged out Martinez, who was right behind him.

Finally, on October 4, 2006, the two-outs-at-the-plate phenomenon came to the post-season. In the second inning of Game 1 of the NLDS between the Dodgers and Mets, with runners on first and second and no outs, the Dodgers' Russell Martin drove a ball off the right-field fence. Shawn Green retrieved it and hit the cutoff man Jose Valentin whose throw home nailed Jeff Kent. After tagging out Kent, catcher Paul Lo Duca heard pitcher John Maine screaming at him to turn around, because J.D. Drew, who started the play on first, was now sprinting down the third base line headed home. Lo Duca spun around and applied the tag to complete another double-play for the ages. Oh, and the Mets won the game 6–5.

The next day's *New York Post* included the following delightful snippet: "There was some debate in the press box whether Dodgers third-base coach Rich Donnelly sent one or both runners. TV replays did not show Donnelly."[31] If Donnelly did indeed send them both, that might seem to qualify as the worse bit of base coaching ever. (Donnelly acknowledged sending Kent, but said that Drew's mad dash caught him by surprise.) But some plays ahead on this list involve coaches doing things that are even worse.

COMMENT

The 1933 double-play at home gives rise to quite the trivia question: When did a Hall of Famer throw to a Hall of Famer to tag out a Hall of Famer and someone else on the same play? Lazzeri, Gehrig, and Goslin all have plaques in Cooperstown. And there are those who think Walker, the one non–Hall of Famer involved in the play, belongs in the Hall.

Incredibly, the 1979 version of the double-play at home was not the only time Gorman Thomas was the second runner caught at the plate on a single play. The next time did not involve the catcher making a double swipe to get two guys in quick succession: It was even more unusual. Stay tuned. (It's a Top Three play.)

The 1985 double-tag at home involved the son of the source of many of baseball's greatest quotes (Yogi Berra) and someone else who may have given the father a run for his money (Ozzie Guillen). Whereas Yogi tended to misspeak, Ozzie was the master of the strange digression, as in this riff: "Sparky Anderson intentionally walked me twice in my career to pitch to Sammy Sosa. Yes, the same Sammy Sosa who hit over 600 home runs—although back then he still had his Jheri curl and was a little darker." On another occasion, Ozzie expressed concern that Michael Jackson's death could adversely affect his team: "I worry about Colon because Colon was a big-time Michael Jackson fan. He might watch the TV and cry all day long. Maybe he's in L.A. at his funeral, because I can't find him. When he gets to Charlotte, Oney [Guillen's son] will call me and say he's there."

Canseco's victimhood in 2000 marks the first of his two appearances in the 150 Most Bizarre Plays, each for a bonehead play. Canseco is an odd duck who had odd things happen to him throughout his career. Just a few days after he headed the ball over the fence to gift the opponent a home run, he asked to be allowed to pitch in a blowout. Be careful what you wish for. He pitched a lousy inning (giving up three runs) and blew out his arm in the process. He was also one of the first major leaguers to warn that steroid use was widespread, but few believed him because he is…. Jose Canseco. He has been convicted of a half-dozen felonies.

One of the least remarked oddities about Canseco involves his identical twin. The careers of Jose and Ozzie Canseco depart from the common outcome when identical twins play professional sports: They're nearly identical. Look at the Niekros, Van Arsdales, Morrises, Bryans, and Sedins. In each case, consistent with what we know about genetics, the identical twins had nearly identical careers. To take just one example, NBA player Tom Van Arsdale played in 929 games, averaging 15.3 points, 4.2 rebounds, and 2.2 assists; brother Dick played in 921 games, averaging 16.4 points, 4.1 rebounds, and 3.3 assists. The Cansecos are outliers. Jose and brother Ozzie combined for 462 home runs. Jose contributed ... 462. Playing parts of three years, Ozzie had 74 plate appearances and never went yard.

98: Cover Your Bases

In the sixth inning of a White Sox–A's game on August 12, 2012, Sox catcher A.J. Pierzynski blasted a home run to break a 1–1 tie. He hit 27 on the season, so no surprise there. But in the next inning Pierzynski did something that would have been remarkable for anyone, and all the more so for a slow-footed catcher. (He stole just 15 bases in a 19-year career and one season grounded into 27 double-plays, tying the record for left-handed batters.) Yet Pierzynski did something never done by Ty Cobb, Rickey Henderson, or any other speedster: He came around to score all the way from first base on a 6–3 (shortstop-to-first) putout without any errors committed by the defense.

Third baseman Adam Rosales and shortstop Cliff Pennington collided while fielding a groundball off the bat of Alexei Ramirez. Pennington withstood the hit and made the throw to first to get Ramirez, but the contact knocked him off balance and kept him from covering third base. Pierzysnki, who was running on the pitch, never stopped as he rounded second and saw third unoccupied. The A's catcher, Derek Norris, saw what was happening and alertly sprinted over to cover the bag, but arrived too late. Because Norris' mad dash left no one covering the plate (the pitcher, Evan Scribner, was hanging out near the mound), Pierzynski scrambled home with the ultimate hustle run, arriving well before the befuddled first baseman, Chris Carter.

COMMENT

Pierzynski's tear around the bases evokes the much more famous play in Game 7 of the 1946 World Series, when Enos Slaughter's "mad dash" from first produced the game-winning run on Harry Walker's single. According to legend, this rare occurrence (a runner scoring from first on a single) stemmed from a combination of Slaughter's amazing speed and Red Sox shortstop Johnny Pesky holding the ball instead of throwing home. This is largely urban legend. Pesky did briefly hesitate before he realized Slaughter was heading home, but the bigger issue from the defensive standpoint is that the Sox's speedy center fielder, Dom DiMaggio, had left the game an inning earlier with a pulled hamstring. DiMaggio was replaced by Leon Culberson, who lacked his speed and arm. More importantly, Slaughter was running on the pitch, and Walker's hit was a gapper. Indeed, it was really a double, not a single. Though it went down in the books as a single, Walker approached second base by the time Slaughter scored. A player who is running on the pitch scoring from first on a double? It is what you'd expect.

None of which is meant to detract from Slaughter, a terrific player. But he was not a speed demon. In his 19-year career, he stole just 71 bases. He was caught 55 times, for a sub-par success rate of 56 percent.

Tricky trivia question: Which player involved in this famous play is part of the only brother combination in which both brothers won batting titles? No, not DiMaggio. Walker—Harry and his more famous brother Dixie. While Joe D. won back-to-back batting titles in 1939 and 1940, brother Dom never came close. The Alous came about as close as you can without achieving the feat. Matty won one batting title, hitting .342 in 1966. Felipe once batted .327 to finish second to ... brother Matty, in 1966.

The Walkers achieved this brotherly feat by the skin of their teeth. Dixie lead the league in hitting only once in his 18-year career: 1944, when he batted .357. It was somewhat of an outlier of a year for him, since his second-best batting average was .319. And he still won the batting average title by a mere two points over Dick Wakefield. Harry Walker also won the title only once, in 1947 when he hit .363—45 points higher than his next best year.

97: Great Act by George Burns

In a Red Sox-Yankees game on June 1, 1923, the Sox looked to pad their 3–0 lead when the first two runners reached base in the eighth inning. George Burns squared to sacrifice, but with the shortstop

Everett Scott trying to hold the runner on second, Burns took advantage of the huge gap and bunted it easily past third baseman Joe Dugan and into left center. By the time centerfielder Whitey Whitt retrieved the ball (Bob Meusel was playing deep in left), two runs scored. An overly ambitious Burns was caught trying to stretch his bunt two-run double into a triple.

COMMENT

The pitcher victimized by the power bunt was Sad Sam Jones, whose 22-year career included two seasons where he won 20 games, two where he lost 20, and a fifth where he led the league in saves (8) while starting 45 games. Jones' lugubrious nickname was bestowed by a sportswriter who thought he always looked downcast. Jones offered an interesting explanation for the dour look: "I would always wear my cap down real low over my eyes. And the sportswriters were more used to fellows like Waite Hoyt, who'd always wear their caps way up so they wouldn't miss seeing any pretty girls."[32]

Burns' bunt off of Sad Sam is a play that wouldn't happen today, because cleanup hitters don't bunt, certainly not with a three-run lead. They didn't make cleanup hitters the same in those days: That year Burns hit just seven home runs. The Yankees' cleanup hitter that day, Wally Pip, hit just six. On the other hand, the Yankees #3 guy, fella named Ruth, slugged 41. (The Red Sox #3 hitter, Mike Menosky, hit *zero*.) By 1923, Babe had begun to change the nature of the game. But it did not change all at once. Consider that Steve Garvey had 33 career sacrifice bunts, including seven in a single season—seven more than Mike Trout has in his career. And Garvey's 33 was exceeded *in a single season* by Frank "Home Run" Baker, who was everyone's idea of a slugger pre–Ruth. Baker led the league in home runs four times and laid down 34 sacrifice bunts in 1914. The Babe himself had 113 career sacrifices, and 14 in 1927, the year he slugged 60 home runs.

Pip had an interesting career in his own right. Though (mis)remembered primarily as the player who sat out a game because of a headache and never returned (since his replacement, Lou Gehrig, played every game for the next 13 years), Pip was actually a slugger and iron man of his own whose career did not suffer from missing the one game. He twice led the American league in home runs and played 150 or more games in six different seasons. When Gehrig took first base

65

from him in 1925, the Yankees sold Pip to the Reds where, in 1926, he played in every game.

Joe Dugan's involvement in the play is reminder of another sensationally bizarre play that cannot be adequately verified. In an article in the *Boston Globe* in 1925, the Yankees' infielder discusses a Philadelphia Athletics victory over the White Sox in 1920—a rare occurrence for the hapless A's.[33] Dugan claims the game came down to the last batter, the Sox's Swede Risberg, with the bases loaded, two out, and the A's leading by 2. Risberg popped a ball that landed fair in between Dugan (playing second base), first baseman Dick Burris, and catcher Cy Perkins. As White Sox raced around the diamond, Perkins frantically returned to the plate where he finally received a throw from Burris. Two White Sox had crossed the plate but the throw was in time to nail the runner from first. Game tied 5–5, headed for the bottom of the ninth. Except Dugan convinced the umpires that the ball had bounced foul by the time Burris retrieved it. Having never reached first base in fair territory, it was a foul ball. Everyone returned to their stations, and Risberg lined out to center to end the game.

Perusing 1920 box scores, it is clear that the game Dugan had in mind was on July 9. That day produced one of the few A's wins against the White Sox, and it ended on a Risberg line drive to center fielder Frank Welch with two runners on base. (The runners happened to be Shoeless Joe Jackson and Buck Weaver, the most sympathetic players thrown out of baseball for throwing the 1919 World Series. They continued playing until Commissioner Kenesaw Mountain Landis banned them in January 1922.) However, the A's led by one run, not two, and the bases were not loaded, so Dugan's description of the play is inexact at best. Quite likely, on the play in question, Jackson scored but Weaver was tagged out, leaving the game tied (as Dugan remembered it). That would leave most of Dugan's account intact. However, because the result of the argument was a foul ball, there is no record of the play in the box score. The dramatic play, culminating in a player convincing an umpire to overturn a ruling, cannot be verified.

96: Multi-Tasking

Play # 116 featured Steve Yeager creamed by a broken bat while in the on-deck circle. It is understandable that Yeager couldn't dodge the bat, because he was so close and not prepared to move. By contrast, we do not expect fielders (except perhaps pitchers) to get hit by bats: They are further away and poised to react. But what if the bat and ball arrive together? That's what happened to A's shortstop Eric Sogard in the seventh inning of a game on August 15, 2013. The broken bat of Astro Chris Carter went exactly the same distance, and in the same direction, as the soft line drive—both right at Sogard. Sogard caught the ball, but the bat struck his ankle and upended him.

Comment

Carter might have broken more bats if the ball found his bat more often: That season, he struck out 213 times, only the fourth player ever to clear the 200 mark. In 2016, he repeated the feat, with 206 Ks.

A player's vulnerability to a broken bat calls to mind the most famous broken bat in baseball history: Mike Piazza's that Roger Clemens picked up and threw at Piazza in Game 2 of the 2000 World Series. Since Piazza obviously did not deliberately send a splintered bat towards the mound, what was Clemens thinking? That question has never been adequately answered, though some suspect Clemens succumbed to a steroid-induced mania. A related question is how Clemens could possibly be allowed to remain in the game (and pitch one of the best games in World Series history) after whirling a dangerous weapon at an opponent for no apparent reason.

95: Batshit Crazy

Similar to Play # 96, but with more elements (and a different outcome). On June 24, 2009, in the second inning of a Red Sox-Nationals game, Elijah Dukes reached base on a bad-hop, broken-bat single—but it was the bat, not the ball, that took the bad hop. Both the top half of Dukes' bat, and the ball, went directly at Sox shortstop Nick Green: the bat airborne, the ball on the ground. The bat dropped just in front of Green, and bounced over his shoulder. He recoiled in self-defense, and thus was in no position to field the ball. It rolled between his legs—a routine grounder turned into a base hit by a bat that played the role of a pulling guard in football. To make the play even more bizarre, the bat became impaled in the outfield grass, standing upright. When Green ran to chase the ball down in shallow left, he had to spread-eagle the bat, barely avoiding the nasty thing for the second time.

COMMENT

Bad hops have twice affected World Series. In Game 7 of the 1924 Series, the Senators trailed the Giants 3–1 in the eighth inning but threatened with runners on second and third. Bucky Walters' routine grounder hit a pebble and leapfrogged third baseman Fred Lindstrom, scoring two runs and tying the game. Amazingly, another bad hop base hit over Lindstrom's head plated the winning run in the twelfth. (Or maybe not so amazing. Maybe the infield was in poor shape, especially around third base.) Thirty-six years later, another World Series Game 7 was affected by a bad hop, this one off the bat of the Pirates' Bill Virdon, with the ball striking Yankee shortstop Tony Kubek in the throat.

If we include the minors, the most consequential bad hop in baseball history occurred in 1905 in the mining town of Rhyolite, Nevada. The Rhyolite team played the team from the nearby town of Beatty on the town field. A ground ball to Rhyolite first baseman, William Griffith, hit something and bounced over his head. Griffith located and pocketed the offending pebble, which looked … interesting. A closer inspection post-game revealed that the "pebble" was a nugget of gold! Griffith prospected the first base area and located a mine shaft that was part of a large deposit of gold. A wire service report passed along this nugget (so to speak): "It is reported that the baseball player has been offered $25,000 for his interest."[34] Griffith benefited less than the industrialist who purchased the mine, someone you may have heard of if you invest in mutual funds: Charles W. Schwab. Some of your assets, dear reader, may trace back to a bad hop single.

94: Mike Throws a Wobbler

On July 18, 2009, just three weeks after the previous play involving a bat taking a bad hop, in the bottom of the sixth inning, after the Dodgers scored on a close play at the plate, the umpire handed a new ball to pitcher Mike Hampton. As the veteran pitcher strolled to the mound, he went to slam the ball into his glove in disgust and … missed. The ball rolled into foul territory, and another Dodgers run scored. Pitchers have slammed balls into their mitt since the days of

Abner Doubleday but, so far as anyone knows, this is the only time the move misfired and led to a run.

COMMENT

I know, I know, Abner Doubleday did not invent baseball. (It remains the case that pitchers slammed balls into their mitts since the days of Doubleday.) Doubleday's *New York Times* obituary does not even mention baseball.[35] The idea of him as baseball's founder is one of those myths with consequences: The Hall of Fame is located in Cooperstown because it was Doubleday's home town.

As for Hampton, he is not the pitcher you would expect to commit a unique defensive blunder. In 2003, he won the Gold Glove, breaking his Braves teammate Greg Maddux's string of 13 straight. Hampton also won the Silver Slugger Award (best hitting pitcher) that year, the first pitcher ever to win those two awards in the same year.

93: Self-Own Hidden Ball Trick

On July 28, 2009, just ten days after Hampton's mishap, in the fifth inning against the Astros, trailing 6–3, the Cubs' Kosuke Fukudome hit a chopper to the mound. The ball bounced inside the shirt of Astros pitcher Jeff Fulchino. Fukudome sprinted to first for the infield hit while Fulchino frantically tried to retrieve the ball from himself.

COMMENT

Two months earlier, the Japanese Fukedome found himself in the middle of a strange controversy. A souvenir stand selling unlicensed Cubs apparel sold a Fukedome jersey displaying the phrase "Horry Kow"—a takeoff on "holy cow," the signature saying of long-time Cubs announcer Harry Caray. The souvenir stand operator reported that the shirt sold well, but some customers complained that it was offensive. The Cubs eventually banned the shirt.

As for Fulchino, maybe it is no accident that he lost a ball in his shirt—he needed an extra large shirt to accommodate his 6'5" 285 pound frame. But when he wasn't losing balls in his uniform, Fulchino fielded well: He committed *zero* errors in a career that spanned 163 games. Admittedly he pitched only 178 innings. Still, consider that Greg Maddux, who won 18 Gold Glove awards, committed 53 errors on his career, or one every 94 innings. Jim Kaat, who won 16 Gold Gloves, committed 56, or one every 81 innings.

92: So Much for the Laws of Physics

On a similar play on June 18, 2006, in the seventh inning against the Mets, Orioles outfielder Ed Rogers charged in to play a base hit by David Wright and the ball somehow ended up stuck in his shirt *behind his back*—another almost impossible variation on the hidden ball trick.

COMMENT

Was Rogers rattled by the play? Who knows, but on the very next play, a base hit to left, he committed his first and only error of the season. One could make a case that Rogers' entertaining mischief rattled the entire team. That inning the Orioles committed three errors, allowed two unearned runs, and watched hopelessly as 48-year-old Julio Franco stole third base.

Rogers had a pretty interesting 2005 as well. Although he was with the Orioles for a while, and appeared in eight games (mostly as a pinch-runner who was caught stealing in both his attempts), he was given just one at-bat. He made the most of it, blasting a two-run home run. For the season, he had an .OBP of 1.000, a slugging percentage of 4.000 and OPS of 5.000.

For his part, David Wright had a fine career cut short by a neck injury. If you look at his season-by-season statistics, you see one season so anomalous that the usual explanation for major fluctuation—random variation—seems unequal to the task. In five of the six seasons from 2004 to 2008 and 2010, Wright was uncannily consistent. His home run totals were 27, 26, 30, 33, and 29. In 2009, however, he slugged just ten (in 535 at-bats). That's what a 93 mph fastball to the head, which Wright experienced early in 2009, can do to a player's confidence and courage at the plate.

91: Ball Within Glove Within Glove

In the second inning of a subway series battle on June 5, 1999, with runners on second and third for the Mets and nobody out, Rey

Ordonez bounced a ground ball to Yankees pitcher, Orlando "El Duque" Hernandez. El Duque fielded the ball but could not get it out of his glove. So he did the natural thing, and tossed the glove (ball firmly inside) to the first baseman, Tino Martinez. Martinez, showing his usual soft hands, caught glove and ball for the unique put-out.

COMMENT

In years since, several players, including pitchers Jon Lester and Terry Mulholland and first baseman Jose Abreu, have done the same thing, throwing the glove and ball as a package to first. El Duque's makes our list of bizarre plays, and the others do not, precisely because they were imitators whereas he improvised. (Also, he is the only one to throw his glove overhand.) Give credit to all the singers who perform covers, but only the songwriter gets the Grammy.

Equaling El Duque in creativity was pitcher Julian Tavaras, who occasionally performed a wacky variation of this play—rolling the ball (as if bowling) to first. Why, you ask? Here was Tavaras' (non)explanation in the *Boston Herald* after first performing this trick in May 2007: "This is what I do. I don't even think about it. I just play and have fun, and I just rolled the ball. You've got to enjoy the game, relax, and some things I just do."[36]

Finally, a shout-out to Anthony Rizzo. On the play in which Jon Lester threw his glove with the ball to first, Rizzo alertly dropped his own glove so as better to catch Lester's.

90: Dancing on the Premises Prohibited

On July 23, 1960, Indians center fielder Jimmy Piersall was ejected by the home plate umpire for doing an elaborate dance. With the Tribe leading 4–2 in the eighth inning against the Red Sox, with a runner on base and Ted Williams at bat, Piersall knew the game hung in the balance. Piersall's dance, right in Williams' line of vision, was designed to distract the Red Sox slugger. Instead, it earned Piersall an early shower.

COMMENT

The ejection was pursuant to Rule 6.04(c): "No fielder shall take a position in the batter's line of vision, and with deliberate unsportsmanlike intent, act in a manner to distract the batter." The rule came about after second baseman Eddie Stanky (fittingly nicknamed "brat") was ejected from a game for doing jumping jacks to distract the batter.

Baseball has seen its share of odd ejections. On August 9, 2009, in Philadelphia, Shane Victorino, like Piersall, was ejected from center field—in this case for arguing balls and strikes. (Victorino's replacement, Jayson Werth, made two errors before the inning was over.) Any discussion of ejections must include Earl Weaver, who was tossed eight times by Ron Luciano alone, before major league baseball stopped assigning Luciano to Orioles games. The Weaver-Luciano feud went back to the minor leagues, where Luciano once ejected Weaver in every game of a four-game series. In the majors, Luciano once ran Weaver in both ends of a doubleheader. Having been ejecting in the first game for protesting a call too ardently, when Weaver brought out the lineup card for the second game, he resumed his beef. Luciano ran him again.

Padres manager Steve Boros was also ejected during a lineup card exchange, in his case for something creative. He brought with him a tape recorder purporting to prove that the ejection of Steve Garvey from the game the day before was a case of mistaken identity: Garvey's teammate, Bip Roberts, uttered the offensive comment. But umpire Charlie Williams ruled that the statute of limitations on Garvey's offense had expired, the recording was hearsay, and Boros was in contempt of court. Something like that.

Adrian Beltre was once ejected for *moving the on-deck circle*. He was standing well off of it, closer to home plate, and when umpire Gerry Davis ordered him to move to the on-deck circle, Beltre instead dragged the on-deck mat to where he was standing. Davis told him to keep moving—to the clubhouse.

On May 11, 1996, the Mets honored their great relief pitcher with John Franco Day. The pre-game ceremony went fine, but the game itself was no feel-good affair. It featured several beanballs and a bench-emptying brawl. Four Mets were ejected from the game on John Franco Day, including, you guessed it, John Franco.

Hall of Fame outfielder Eddie Roush was actually tossed from a game for falling asleep. When a long argument took place in the infield, Roush lay down on the outfield grass and dozed off. When play returned, he proved difficult to rouse. By the time he had awakened, umpire Barry McCormick had ejected him for delay of game.

A game in 1938 produced a *voluntary* ejection. Cleveland's starting pitcher Johnny Allen liked to wear a tee-shirt with a torn sleeve under his sweatshirt. When batters complained that the sleeve was distracting, umpire Bill McGowan ordered Allen to change shirts. Allen stormed off the field and refused to return.

The colorful Stanley "Frenchy" Bordagaray was not only suspended for 60 days for spitting at an umpire, but also fined $500 (which was quite a lot in 1936). Asked whether he thought the penalty too severe, Bordagaray let on that it was "more than I expectorated."[37]

The all-time leader for ejections is Bobby Cox with 161. Many of those ejections came when Cox was shielding his players from ejection. On one such occasion, he failed to keep Jeff Francoeur from getting himself tossed. The two headed to the clubhouse together. Francoeur told the *Atlanta Constitution* about their conversation when they arrived: "I'm like, 'What do I do?' He said, 'Go have a couple cold beers and get in the cold tub or something and relax. And then you'll probably have to write a $500 check. Or you can do what I do, write a $10,000 check and tell them when it runs out, let me know.'"[38] (Cox was the subject of the strangest quote attributed to one of baseball's strangest owners, Ted Turner. At a press conference after firing Cox, Turner was asked who was on his short list to replace Cox. He replied, "It would be Bobby Cox if I hadn't just fired him. We need someone like him around here."[39])

Finally, let's return to the man whose ejection for jumping jacks sparked the discussion of strange ejections: Jimmy Piersall. There was nothing funny about Piersall's struggle with mental illness, and it is difficult to know where his colorful personality left off and the demons began. We do know that Piersall did odd things on the diamond. He once stepped up to bat wearing a Beatles wig and playing air guitar on his bat. He celebrated his 100th career home run by running the bases backwards. And when the bullpen cart bringing in a relief pitcher would pass him in the outfield, Piersall would stick out his thumb to hitch a ride. Not everyone found such antics amusing. His banishment for dancing to distract Ted Williams was Piersall's sixth ejection of the 1960 season. His eventual total of seven tied the record for most ejections in a season by Johnny Evers, the shortstop of Tinkers to Evers to Chance and Merkle's Boner fame.

89: Pitcher Throws Ball Away

On August 20, 2009, in the fourth inning of the Red Sox-Blue Jays game, with Jason Bay on first and David Ortiz at bat, catcher Rod Barajas' toss back to the mound got past pitcher Brett Cecil. Cecil scrambled to retrieve the ball near second base before the runners could advance. So far, so good. Then Cecil held up the scuffed ball, signaling the home plate umpire that he wanted a new one. But the flustered pitcher did not request time out, nor throw the ball home for the exchange. Instead, he tossed it into the Jays' dugout. Bay was awarded third for this gratuitous throwing error (E-1—"pitcher's decision to remove live ball from game"), the most effortless two-base advance in baseball history.

COMMENT

It was Cecil's only error that season. Seven times in his ten-year career, Cecil committed exactly one error, and the other three seasons zero. Good field, no hit. Because he played eight of his ten seasons in the American League, Cecil rarely batted. All told, he came to the plate seven times, striking out six and never reaching base.

Cecil, a left-handed pitcher, does everything else with his right hand. Maybe he dreamed at a young age of being a pitcher, where being a southpaw is an advantage. For a field player, of course, the ideal is to bat left (and thus start closer to first base) and throw right (and thus be eligible to play any position). There are numerous ballplayers who fit this mold, no doubt some of whom at a young age, at the suggestion of a parent or coach, trained themselves to bat left and/or throw right, for this very reason. By contrast, few players in major league history got things backwards and threw left while hitting right. By far the best was someone known to march to a different drummer: Rickey Henderson.

88: Three-Ring Circus

On July 31, 1982, in the bottom of the first inning against the Indians, the Brewers had Robin Yount on second base and Gorman

Thomas on first. Ben Oglivie lined out to second baseman Larry Milbourne. Milbourne threw to first to try and double off Thomas, but his throw got past first-baseman Mike Hargrove. Hargrove retrieved the ball and threw home to try and catch Young, but his wild throw got past catcher Chris Bando. Bando chased it down near the dugout and threw to third to try and nail the advancing Thomas. However, *his* wild throw sailed into left field, allowing Thomas to score. At the time Milbourne made the catch, there were two outs and runners on first and second, and a chance to end the inning if he made a good throw to first. *Three* wild throws later, the Indians had two runs.

COMMENT

Hargrove, whose first inning home run gave the Indians a lead they lost thanks to the procession of bad throws, enjoyed one of the great nicknames in baseball, courtesy of his habit of stepping out of the batter's box and going through a long routine after every pitch: "The Human Rain Delay." A solid player for eleven years, the Human Rain Delay amassed a mediocre record as a manager for three teams. In 2007, he stepped down as manager of the Mariners even though the team was riding an eight-game winning streak and was 12 games over .500. Despite much speculation about his departure, the mystery was never resolved. According to the Elias Baseball Bureau, it was the first time in over a century that a manager quit during a winning streak of eight or more games—a weird stat, for sure, but weird behavior too.

Robin Yount, who scored the first run thanks to the Indians' generosity, also suffered some bad luck that season. Going into the last game of the season, he was batting .328, four points behind Willie Wilson for the league lead. Wilson sat out his team's finale, so Yount needed four hits to nose out Wilson for the batting title. He slammed two homers and a triple in his first four at-bats, and came up in the ninth inning needing one more hit to squeak past Wilson by .0005. He was hit by a pitch. Ouch.

Yount did win the American League MVP, so it is hard to feel too sorry for him, but even then he received a smidgen of bad luck. He should have been the unanimous winner, hands down. He received 27 of 28 first place votes, with one voter opting for Reggie Jackson, who finished sixth in the voting overall. Jackson hit 39 home runs to

Yount's 29, but Yount, an excellent defensive shortstop, easily out-paced Jackson in every other category—batting average, on-base percentage, slugging percentage, doubles, triples, runs scored, runs batted in, you name it. The one dissenter, a Toronto writer, explained to UPI that Jackson had the ability to carry a team by himself.[40] But that season, Jackson was arguably not even the best player on the California Angels (Doug DeCinces finished ahead of him in the MVP voting), and the Angels won fewer games than Yount's Brewers.

If Yount experienced mild misfortune in not winning unanimously, and just missing out on a batting title, he was not even close to the unluckiest ballplayer in his own family. His brother Larry, a pitcher, made his major league debut on September 15, 1971, for the Astros. After a few warm-up tosses, his elbow hurt and he came out. Yount was sent to the minors, where he remained for several years before retiring. Because he was officially announced into the game, the record books record him as having played. Larry Yount is the only pitcher in major league history to have faced zero batters.

87: *Great Move by Elvis*

On August 20, 2013, with the Astros batting in the fifth inning against the Rangers with one out and Max Stassi at first, Marwin Gonzalez's chopper was speared by pitcher Jason Frasor. Frasor's throw to second sailed over the head of shortstop Elvis Andrus towards centerfield, where second baseman Ian Kinsler, alertly backing up, snared the ball on the fly. Andrus nevertheless brought his glove down to tag Stassi, fooling Stassi into thinking he was tagged out. Stassi started toward the dugout, and before coaches or teammates could get his attention, Kinsler charged in and tagged him out for real.

COMMENT

Kinsler's first major league at bat was a base hit against Curt Shilling; his last was a home run. Stassi, his victim on this play, also had a strong start to his career, sort of. He had two hits in his first game, and notched his first RBI in his second game the hard way—with the bases loaded, he was struck in the face by a 96 mile per hour fastball from Tanner Scheppers. That pretty much ended Stassi's rookie season. His seven-year career as a part-time player produced what we might call a catcher's double double—zero triples, zero stolen bases. In fact, zero stolen base attempts.

Elvis Andrus, the man who deked Stassi, either was or was not named after Elvis Presley. Here is what he told the *New York Times*: "I asked my mother a lot of times, but she never told me. Maybe my dad liked Elvis Presley. I'm not sure about that."[41]

86: Penalty Declined

On June 5, 1990, the Pirates' Bobby Bonilla could have been awarded first base on catcher's interference when, in the first inning, his bat grazed the glove of Cubs catcher Joe Girardi. However, notwithstanding his impeded swing, Bonilla launched the ball over the fence for a three-run home run. The Pirates declined the catcher's interference, opting for the three runs instead.

COMMENT

Yes, catcher's interference may be declined. Rule 6.08c: "...If a play follows the (catcher's) interference, the manager of the offense may advise the plate umpire that he elects to decline the interference penalty and accept the play."

Bonilla had a fine career, slugging 287 home runs over 16 seasons and earning six all-star selections. Still, not the sort of player to have his special day recognized by fans annually. For some reason, when the Mets released Bonilla in 2000, the club agreed to pay him $1.19 million every year from 2011 through 2035. The payments are made each July 1, which unamused Met fans still refer to as Bobby Bonilla Day.

85: Some People Are Never Satisfied

A similar play on September 15, 2009, receives a slightly higher ranking because of an additional bizarre element. In the ninth inning, the Yankees' Mark Teixeira belted a ball off the centerfield wall, and managed to reach third even though, as he ran to first, he turned back to yell at the home plate umpire that his bat hit the glove of catcher Mike Napoli. As Vernon Wells attempted the catch, his foot became wedged in the wall and his shoe came off. Teixeira coasted into third with his first triple in two years.

COMMENT

Spoiler alert: We're not quite done with strange plays involving catcher's interference. It is, of course, a rare occurrence, but Jacoby Ellsbury managed to reach by way of catcher's interference twelve times in a single season (2016). How rare is that? No one else in baseball had more than three that year, and before Ellsbury the record for a season was eight. Ellsbury reached on catcher's interference thirty times in his career, also a record. He stands in the back of the batter's box, and his unusual swing brings the bat back far, but you would think word would have gotten around and catchers backed up a bit—especially since the speedy Ellsbury was not a guy you wanted to gift first base to.

Ellsbury's career statistics include one other oddity: his entire 2011 season. In his first three seasons, 2007–2009, he combined for just 20 home runs in almost 1300 at-bats. In 2010, when injuries reduced him to 78 at-bats, Ellsbury hit *zero* round-trippers. The next season, he exploded for 34. Ellsbury drove in 105 runs, dwarfing his previous high of 60, and, for good measure, batted .321. He finished second in the American League MVP voting. This from a guy who had never hit more than seven home runs in a season *in the minor leagues.*

This was past the steroid era, so maybe just a case of a 27-year-old finally reaching his potential (albeit all at once)? Except look what happened after Ellsbury's one dream season. In 2012, injuries limited him to 323 at-bats, and he hit just four home runs while his batting average dropped 50 points. Over the next five years, he cracked double figures in home runs only once, and that was just 16. He never again remotely approached that 2011 peak. But he did up his game in at least one respect: drawing catcher's interference.

84: Tommy and the Terrible, Horrible, No Good, Very Bad Play

On July 27, 1988, with the Brewers' Jim Gantner on first and one out in the fourth inning, Yankees pitcher Tommy John fielded a slow ground ball off the bat of Jeffrey Leonard. The 45-year-old John (in his *25th* season) bobbled the ball and dropped it, as a result of which he had no play on Leonard. He nevertheless elected to make a pointless throw to first but the ball sailed way wide of first-baseman Don

Mattingly and into right field. Dave Winfield fielded the ball and uncorked a perfect throw home that seemed destined to nail Gantner, but John cut the ball off and threw to third to try and get Leonard instead. His throw sailed into the third base dugout, scoring Leonard. When the dust cleared, the Brewers had two runs on a routine groundball to the mound and John was credited with three errors (in twelve seconds). And the official scoring did not fully capture John's futility on the play: Cutting off Winfield's throw was the single most boneheaded thing he did, yet did not go down as an error.

COMMENT

It used to be part of the received baseball wisdom that a nineteenth-century New York Giants third baseman named Mike Grady committed five or six errors on a play. Baseball historian Bill Deane debunked that notion in his fine book, *Baseball Myths: Debating, Debunking and Disproving Tales from the Diamond.* No one has ever committed four errors on a play, and only Tommy John managed three.[42] There are only a few instances of a team committing three errors on a play, let alone a single player.

To say this play was uncharacteristic for John is gross understatement. In his 26-year career, there were only nine times he committed three errors *in an entire season.* In twelve different seasons, he committed *zero* errors. On that one play in July 1988, however, he supplied some memorable defense. Not that it hurt him much—the Yankees won the game 16–3, nothing John career win 285. He would end up with 288. The failure to get 12 more seems to have cost him the Hall of Fame, an instance of voters' silly devotion to round numbers.

John achieved baseball immortality nonetheless, by way of the pioneering elbow surgery that came to be named after him and that made possible his very long career.

83: *That's Using Your Head*

This one you've seen. On May 26, 1993, in the fourth inning the Indians' Carlos Martinez lifted a ball to deep right field. The Rangers' Jose Canseco tracked the ball down and reached up for the catch, but somehow fanned. The ball plunked him on the head and looped over the fence for a home run.

COMMENT

In the immediate aftermath, centerfielder David Hulse strolled over to commiserate with Canseco and the two of them openly laughed. The Rangers lost the game 7–6, the margin of Canseco's blooper. (It did not help that Canseco was caught stealing in the eighth, with the Rangers down two.) But you can't blame Hulse and Canseco for laughing. One loss in May will be long forgotten. The head-assisted home run never will be.

It doesn't make the Most Bizarre Plays list, which is limited to major league games, but Miguel Sano experienced something similar to Canseco in a Triple A game. Playing third base during a rehab stint with the Rochester Red Wings, Sano camped under a sky-high infield fly that he apparently lost in the sun. What makes this play extra cool is that, after the ball bopped Sano in the head, his teammate, third baseman James Beresford, alertly made a diving catch before the ball touched down.

High pop-ups in the infield are harder to catch than they seem. (They tend to have backspin that outfield flies lack.) Believe it or not, Alex Rodriguez refused to go for high flies if at all possible. He'd scamper out of the way and let the shortstop come make the catch.

As for Carlos Martinez, the recipient of Canseco's headed home run, thanks to that gift he had five homers that season. The year before, he also had five. The year before that? Five. The two years before that? Four and five. In those five years, his RBI totals were 32, 24, 30, 35, 31. Talk about consistency.

82: Chaplin-esque Home Run

On September 29, 2012, with the bases loaded in the first inning against the Cardinals, the Nationals' Michael Morse blasted a ball that seemed to bounce off the top of the right-field wall in Busch stadium and return to the playing field. Cardinals right fielder Carlos Beltran retrieved the ball and threw it to the infield. The runners held up to see if the ball might be caught, causing such a backlog on the bases that Morse was caught in a rundown and tagged out trying to return to first. Replay review, however, showed that the ball cleared the fence for a home run (before hitting a back wall that is out of play). Morse lingered at first base during the lengthy review process, figuring that, after the umpires signaled home run, he would have to complete his trot. After all, a home run is not a home run until a player touches all the bases.

Except, for some reason, after reversing the call and declaring the ball a home run, the umpires instructed Morse to return to home plate to begin his trot anew. After obeying and returning to the plate, Morse pantomimed a swing and home run before rounding the bases. Nats announcer Bob Carpenter got in the spirit, giving a vigorous call of Morse's imaginary new hit: "There it goes. Right field, it is deep! See. You. Later. Grand Slam, the Nationals are on top by four."

COMMENT

All baseball history books should include Babe Ruth, and a legendary home run is a good excuse to bring in Babe lore. While everyone knows that Ruth was an all-star pitcher before being unleashed on the American League as an outfielder, it is less well-known that he pitched in a perfect game. Pitched *in* a perfect game is not the same thing as pitching a perfect game.

On June 23, 1917, against the Senators, Ruth walked the first batter, Ray Morgan. Babe argued ball four so strenuously that he was ejected. Ernie Shore was brought in to replace him, obviously unprepared for such an early appearance. Shore received a break when, on his first pitch, Morgan was thrown out attempting to steal. Shore proceeded to retire the next 26 batters, for a perfect game ... if you don't count the batter Ruth walked. His 1980 obituary in the *New York Times* was headlined: "Ernie Shore; Pitched A Rare Perfect Game After Relieving Ruth."[43]

Incidentally, Ruth was so incensed by the ejection that he charged home plate umpire Brick Owens and slugged him with a left hook, prompting a policeman to escort Babe from the field. He drew a ten-game suspension for the punch. He, along with Shore, was also credited with a "combined no-hitter," surely not one of the Babe's greatest accomplishments. In a sign of how the times were different, Shore struck out just two batters during his masterpiece. His counterpart, Washington's Doc Ayers, pitched a complete game and struck out *zero*. Sixty-one batters came to the plate and 58 put the ball in play.

81: Stuck on You

On April 6, 2017, pinch-hitting to lead off the seventh inning, Chicago Cubs outfielder Matt Szczur struck out on a pitch in the dirt. Cardinals catcher Yadier Molina blocked the pitch, and sought to retrieve the ball while Szczur raced to first base. Szczur reached safely because Molina's frantic search to locate the ball was unsuccessful. That's because Molina did not think to look on his chest protector, where the ball was stuck. How that happened remains a mystery, since Velcro is not part of a catcher's equipment.

COMMENT

Molina vehemently objected to the suggestion that he puts pine tar on his chest protector, but could offer no explanation for the mishap. The play may have shaken up the pitcher, Brett Cecil, whom we last encountered absent-mindedly tossing a live ball into the dugout. After Szczur reached, Cecil walked John Jay, allowed a home run to Kyle Schwarber, walked Kris Bryant, and yielded a single to Anthony Rizzo. By the time he was mercifully removed, the Cubs had turned a 4–2 deficit into a lead they would not lose. And it all started because a ball fastened itself to Yadier Molina's chest protector.

There are Molinas all over this book because there are Molinas all over baseball. Yadier, along with brothers Jose and Bengie, were all outstanding defense catchers with long major league careers. Of the nineteen three-brother combinations in MLB history, only the DiMaggios (Joe, Dom, Vince) and Alous (Felipe, Matty, Jesus) approach the Molinas. Which combination is best makes for a nice barroom argument. The DiMaggios combined for 573 home runs, easily surpassing the Molinas (339) and Alous (269) but the Alous have the most hits (5,094 to DiMaggios' 4,853 and Molinas' 3,872). The Molinas combined for seven Gold Gloves and all three Molinas wear World Series rings, the only set of three brothers to achieve that distinction.

80: Easiest Run of His Life

Speaking of the Molinas.... On September 26, 2008, in the sixth inning against the Dodgers, Giants catcher Bengie clobbered a ball that appeared to bounce off the top of the fence. The notoriously slow Molina settled for a single. Bruce Bochy sent in Emmanuel Burris as a pinch-runner. Less than a month earlier, Commissioner Bud Selig had implemented instant replay review of possible home runs. When the review determined that Molina's drive had cleared the fence, the umpires reversed the call and awarded Molina a home run. However, Burris had officially entered the game for Molina and, after a long consultation with both managers, the umpires determined that the substitution could not be undone. Accordingly, Burris completed the home run trot. Molina was awarded the home run and RBI, but Burris credited with the run scored.

COMMENT

Of course, the Giants were not amused that Molina had to be removed from what was (thanks to his home run) a tie game. Wouldn't you know it, in the bottom of the ninth with the Giants trailing by a run, Molina's replacement, Steve Colm, drove in the tying run, and the Giants went on to win in the tenth.

For Burris, it was his second home run trot in less than a month—just three weeks earlier, he hit his first career home run. And last career home run. Burris went yard once in a seven-year career spanning 325 games and 768 at-bats. For the non–dead ball era, that is an impressive (non)accomplishment. But it does not approach the achievement of infielder Duane Kuiper who managed exactly one home run in ten years and 3,259 at bats. The homer came in 1977 (off future Cy Young winner, Steve Stone). The next year, Kuiper had two bases loaded triples *in one game*—one of just three players in MLB history to accomplish that feat. Go figure.

 # 79: Walker on Broken Glass

On May 30, 1946, in the nightcap of a doubleheader at Ebbets Field, in the top of the second inning of a 2–2 game, a Boston Braves player named Carvel Williams "Bama" Rowell slammed a long fly-ball off the Bulova clock on the scoreboard in right field. The ball shattered the clock's glass, whose fragments rained down on Dodgers right fielder Dixie Walker. Withstanding the assault, Walker retrieved the ball and held Rowell to a double.

Comment

The shattered glass may have shaken up the Dodgers. While club personnel cleaned up the glass, manager Leo Durocher summoned a new pitcher, the hard throwing Rex Barney. Barney issued an intentional walk, then three unintentional walks, and departed. In came Art Herring, who was greeted with a bases-clearing triple by Skippy Roberge—one of just two triples in Oberge's three-year career. By the time the dust cleared, the Braves had seven runs on three hits, one of which—Rowell's clock-shattering double—has been immortalized. (See below.)

The four consecutive walks was not *that* unusual for the notoriously wild Barney. On September 9, 1948, before 36,000 rabid fans at the Polo Grounds, against the rival Giants, Barney got off to a rough start. He walked the first batter on four pitches. With one out, he fielded a bouncer and committed a throwing error. Now, with runners on first and third, he walked another batter—loading the bases solely through his generosity. But Barney induced a double-play ball to escape unscathed, and set down the next 24 batters for a no-hit shutout.

Rowell's clock-shattering hit may have inspired the scene in Bernard Malumud's novel *The Natural* (published four years later) in which Roy Hobbs slugs a home run that shatters a clock and "spattered minutes all over the place." Incidentally, Bulova promised a watch to any player who hit the clock, but did not make good on the payment to Walker until 1989 when sportswriter Bert Sugar learned about this injustice. The stubborn company insisted that its offer of a watch did not constitute a binding contract, but under pressure from Sugar it relented. In a ceremony marking "Bama Rowell Day" in the player's home town of Citronelle, Alabama, Rowell finally received the watch he earned 41 years earlier.

 # 78: Bat and Ball Can't Get Enough of Each Other

On September 23, 2008, with the Mets trailing the Cubs 2–0 in the fifth inning, with a runner on first and one out, the Cubs expected Johan Santana to bunt. Santana faked a bunt, then slapped a groundball in the direction of Cubs pitcher Sean Marshall. However, part of Santana's broken bat flew toward Marshall as well. Distracted by the bat, Marshall let the ball get past him, but shortstop Ronny Cedeno was in position to field it until the ball struck the bat a second time, this time behind the mound! The second bat-on-ball altered the flight of the ball so that Cedeno could not make the play.

COMMENT

Aided by this unique base hit, the Mets scored two runs in the inning to tie the game and went on to win 6–2. Santana pitched a gem to notch his 15th win, lasting eight innings and throwing 125 pitches. That wasn't his career high for pitches in a game. That would come four years later, and is a source of controversy.

For at least a quarter century, teams have taken pitch counts seriously, often limiting starting pitchers to 100 or fewer pitches in a game. Old-timers, and even some new-timers, complain about these artificial restrictions, as a result of which complete games, once routine, have become increasingly rare. Santana, for example, though one of the best pitchers in the game for years, completed just 15 games in his career. In 2012, the Mets allowed him to throw 134 pitches because he had a no-hitter. Santana completed the no-no—to this day, the only no-hitter in Mets history. But he was never the same. He struggled mightily the rest of the 2012 season. (The no-hitter lowered his ERA to 2.38. It ended up 4.85.) The following spring training Santana suffered an arm injury, and never returned to the major leagues. Coincidence?

If not, Santana's career was ruined by good luck. In the sixth inning of the no-hitter, a line drive by Carlos Beltran clearly hit the chalk past the third-base bag, only to be called foul. The bad call preserved Santana's no-hitter, but also kept him in the game much longer than he normally would have pitched.

Santana always maintained that he has no regrets about staying in the game past his arm's expiration date. His likely tradeoff of one-game glory at the expense of several more years of pitching calls to mind Steve Stone's 1980 season. Throwing an inordinate number of curve balls (his best pitch but hard on the arm), Stone won 25 games and the Cy Young Award. The next year he went 4–7, injured his arm, and was through. Stone always maintained that the Cy Young season shortened his career but was worth it.

#77: Oops, He's Already Out

With the bases loaded and one out in the eleventh inning against the Brewers on June 10, 2016, the Mets' Matt Reynolds hit a line-drive at shortstop Jonathan Villar, who dropped it. Though the muff was not deliberate, it was not necessarily bad for the Brewers: It made possible an inning-ending double-play. When Villar flipped to Scooter Gennett for the force out at second, Gennett's obvious move was to throw to first to get Reynolds. Gennett chose instead to chase Kelly Johnson, who started the play at first and was now in between first and second. He ran down Johnson and tagged him for what he thought was a double-play. Just one problem: Johnson was the runner already out on the force play at second base. He could not be out twice on the same play. The winning run scored on the non-double-play.

COMMENT

Almost one year to the day of his costly blunder, Gennett became the seventeenth player in MLB history to hit four home runs in a game. Later in the 2017 season, he became the answer to a bizarre trivia question: Who are the two players in baseball history to hit their twentieth home run in a game they pitched? The other answer is not surprising: Babe Ruth. But what was Gennett doing pitching on August 14, 2017? Surely, it wasn't so he could share a silly distinction with Babe Ruth. No, he pitched the eighth inning to spare the bullpen: The Reds had already used five pitchers and trailed by eight runs. Speaking of the number eight, Gennett had an eventful eighth inning: He hit a two-run home run in the top of the eighth and gave up a two-run homer (to Javy Baez) in the bottom.

That Ruth is the other player to pitch on the day he hit his twentieth homer is actually less obvious than one might think. After all, didn't Babe stop pitching when he became a full-time outfielder? Not right away. In what may be Ruth's least appreciated seasons, his last two with the Red Sox, 1918 and 1919, he both pitched (winning 22 games combined) and played a fair amount of outfield (hitting 40 home runs combined).

Exactly 100 years later, in 2018, Shohei Ohtani became the first player since Ruth to pitch 50 innings and hit 15 home runs in a season. Ohtani started only 10 games on the mound, going 4–2 with a solid ERA of 3.31. In 1918, Ruth started 20 games and finished 13–7 with a 2.22 Era. Advantage Babe. At bat, however, Ohtani held his own in comparison with Ruth. In 317 at-bats, Babe batted. 300, swatted 11 home runs and drove in 61 runs. In 326 at bats, Ohtani batted .285, hit 22 home runs and the identical 61 RBIs. Advantage Ohtani (though it should be noted that Babe produced those numbers during the dead ball era). Like Scooter Gennett, Ohtani is in special company.

76: *The Amazing Randy*

Here is another one you've seen: On March 24, 2001, in the seventh inning of a spring training game between the Diamondbacks and Giants, a Randy Johnson fastball roughly three fourths of the way to the plate encountered and dismantled a most unfortunate dove. The bird's remains scattered near home plate.

COMMENT

The ballfield killing was not unprecedented. On August 4, 1983, a practice throw between innings by Yankees outfielder Dave Winfield struck and killed a seagull in Toronto. Johnson's kill was more impressive because it caused the victim to explode, but Winfield's had a stranger aftermath. After the game, he was escorted to a Toronto Police station and charged with causing "unnecessary suffering of an animal" under Section 402.1(a) of Canada's Criminal Code, punishable by six months in prison or a $500 fine. Eventually the authorities determined that Winfield lacked criminal intent, and dropped charges. The incident is best remembered, or at least should be, for the assessment of Yankees manager Billy Martin: "That's the first time Winfield hit the cutoff man all year."[44]

Even if he missed cutoff men, Winfield was arguably the best all-around athlete in baseball history. He was, of course, an easy choice for the Hall of Fame, having been a superb five-tool player his entire career. At the University of Minnesota, he not only excelled at the plate and in the field, but also on the mound. He also starred on the Gopher basketball team that won the Big Ten his senior year. The Padres, the NBA's Atlanta Hawks, and the ABA's Utah Stars all drafted him. As did the NFL's Minnesota Vikings, even though Winfield did not play college football.

87

The batter when Johnson murdered the bird, Calvin Murray, made it into our list of Most Bizarre Plays just by standing at the plate with the bat on his shoulders. But he also earned his way onto the list for a play in which the one thing he did not do was stay on his feet. Stay tuned.

75: *Randle Blows It*

This is another one that will catch few people by surprise because most fans have seen it 100 times. On May 27, 1981, in the sixth inning the Royals' Amos Otis hit a swinging bunt down the third base line, a sure hit unless the ball rolled foul. It looked like it would stay fair, until Mariners third baseman Lenny Randle got down on all fours and blew it foul.

COMMENT

During the 1980s, while playing with the Mariners, Randle moon-lighted as a stand-up comic. On this play, he did lie-down comedy. But blowing on the baseball provided comic relief only; Otis was awarded first base. Is there actually a rule governing what Randle did? Not exactly. But the umpires invoked two rules. Rule 7.09 calls *base runner* interference on a player who "interferes with" a batter or thrown ball. Rule 901(c) says "each umpire has authority to rule on any point not specifically covered in these rules." Combining the spirit of Rule 7.09 with the vast discretion given by Rule 9.01, umpire Larry McCoy awarded Otis first base.

Kansas City third baseman Kevin Seitzer is the rare person who never saw the Randle play. Either that or, in the heat of the moment, he forgot. He tried the Randle Blow in a game six years later. Only this time the ball refused to obey, and Seitzer finally snatched it up in disgust in fair territory.

In a game in 1972, an umpire allegedly waved a *bat* foul. The bat flew out of the hands of the Yankees' Bobby Murcer and bounced near the first-base line, spun around a bit, and settled in foul territory. Ron Luciano, the colorful umpire who was umpiring first, gave a flamboyant foul call. The league fined him for conduct unbecoming an umpire. At any rate, that is a story Luciano liked to tell. I've been unable to verify it, and Luciano was capable of tall tales. But this one rings true. Who would think to make up such a thing?

74: Lucky Bill Buckner

People associate Bill Buckner with his historic error in Game 6 of the 1986 World Series. But Buckner occasionally got lucky. On April 25, 1990, in the fourth inning with the Red Sox trailing the Angels 1–0, the oft-injured 40-year-old drilled a ball over the head of right fielder Claudell Washington. Back by the fence Washington leaped for it, missed, and did a head-over-heels somersault into the right field stands. As the ball lay unattended near the wall, Buckner could have walked around the bases. By the time Buckner hobbled home, Washington still had not returned to the playing field.

COMMENT

The day was not completely lucky for Buckner and the Red Sox. They managed 13 hits and 18 base runners but scored only the one run provided by Buckner, and fell 3–1. It was the last home run and only inside-the-park home run of Buckner's 22-year career.

Does it seem surprising that Buckner was still with the Red Sox in 1990, four years after his error made him a reviled figure in Beantown? Actually, "still" and "reviled" are both misleading. The Sox traded Buckner in '87, but reacquired him as a free agent before the '90 season. It might seem crazy for Buckner to choose to finish his career in Boston, and for the club to saddle Sox fans with the last person they wanted to be reminded of. But it is at least part myth that Red Sox fans were brutal to Buckner, hating on him so much that they drove him far away (to Idaho) in retirement. Two days after the Sox lost the '86 World Series, in a parade to commemorate their great season, thousands of fans gave Bucker a one-minute ovation. So too, on Opening Day in '90, during player introductions the fans greeted him with a standing ovation.

It wasn't just the fans who forgave Buckner. It seems safe to assume that the Red Sox management reacquired him as much as an expression of good will as anything else. He was, by this point, a broken down 40-year-old who, the previous season with the Royals, batted .216 with 1 home run in 178 at-bats. (For the Red Sox, on the second go round, he played in 22 games, batting .186 with the one inside-the-park home run.)

73: A Good Wind Would Blow Him Away

On July 11, 1961, in the ninth inning of the 1961 all-star game, Stu Miller committed a balk when the wind in Candlestick Park blew him off the mound. That, at any rate, is how history has recorded the play. The less dramatic reality is that the wind caused Miller to sway, resulting in the balk. Miller stood 5'11" and weighed just 149 pounds, and the winds are gusty in Frisco. Still, many a game has been played with swirling winds and, so far as I can tell, the wind-assisted balk remains unique in the annals of baseball history.

COMMENT

It did not look like an all-star game in the ninth inning when, in addition to Miller's balk, the National League committed two errors—and five in the game (though they won 5–4). Miller later recalled that "the wind was really blowin' up a storm.... Just as I went into my motion, a real whoosh came and I swayed."[45] He ruefully remarked that "my feet didn't move, so I didn't get blown off the mound as the story goes. Each time it gets told, I get blown farther off the mound." Stu Miller meet baseball lore. In fact, it gets worse. Miller struck out the side in the tenth inning to earn the win for the National League, but that part has been forgotten. Meanwhile, while everyone remembers Miller, long forgotten is the performance in that game of Ken Boyer, who made two errors, one of them in the fateful ninth when the American League scored three runs to tie the game. Then in the bottom of the ninth, with the score tied, Boyer was picked off first.

Incidentally, in those days there were two all-star games each year. In the second one, just three weeks later, Miller pitched brilliantly, allowing just one base runner while striking out five in three innings. The game was tied 1–1 after nine, when rain brought it to an end—the first tie in all-star history. The next and last (to date) was in 2002, when the 7–7 game was called after eleven innings when the teams ran out of pitchers.

For the record, in the first 14 years of his career, Stu Miller committed exactly one balk (not counting the all-star game). But in the 15th year, as a 39-year-old pitching for the Orioles in 1967, he committed two. I am aware of no explanation.

72: Forget Something?

On August 13, 2018, during the fourth inning against the Indians, Reds pitcher Homer Bailey literally went through the motions of a pitch to Greg Allen. Partway through the delivery, Bailey realized he was missing something—the ball was still in his glove. The balk allowed the runners, Jan Gomes and Jason Kipnis, to advance a base.

COMMENT

I give this play the nod over Stu Miller's balk because Miller had a bit of an excuse. As for Bailey, it was not only a tough pitch, but a tough game (he was bombed and the Reds lost 10–3) and a brutal season, a candidate for the worst in baseball history. He finished with a record of 1–14 and an ERA over 6. While it is hard to equal that record for futility, the Pirates' John Van Benschoten may have managed. In 2007, Van Benschoten was 0–7 with an ERA of 10.15.

For his career, Van Benschoten was 3–13 with an ERA of 9.20. Sadly, he had been a highly-regarded prospect. At Kent State, Van Benschoten was not only a terrific pitcher but also a feared slugger who one season blasted 31 home runs. The Pirates decided his destiny was on the mound, and made him the eighth overall pick in the 2001 draft. Did they make a mistake by not playing him in the field instead? Not necessarily. In his limited time at the plate (21 at-bats), Van Benschoten batted .095. Some talented athletes simply aren't meant for the show.

71: Triple Steal

There have been several triple steals, because in the early days of the game a steal of home was surprisingly common. Believe it or not, a triple steal also happened in the modern game. On May 27, 2008, in the sixth inning, the Indians, leading 5–2, had the bases loaded against the White Sox, with David Dellucci on third, Grady Sizemore on second, and Jamey Carroll on first. White Sox pitcher Ehren Wassermann attempted the play that never works: Faking a throw to third and then throwing to first. Except this time it *did* work, catching Carroll off the bag. But as first baseman Paul Konerko chased Carroll toward second, Dellucci broke home. Konerko's throw was off-line. Dellucci scored, Sizemore advanced to third and Carroll to second.

COMMENT

All three runners were generously awarded stolen bases. (The play could have been scored an error on Konerko and/or fielder's choice.) Wasserman is surely the only pitcher in baseball history who allowed three steals on one play but never allowed a home run in his career (spanning 57 games and 42 innings). Of course, he is one of the very few pitchers to allow three steals on one play period. Which shows how unfair statistics can be: The only thing Wasserman did on the play was pick a runner off first!

Speaking of misleading statistics, being the middle runner on a triple steal is as cheap a stolen base as you can get. But Sizemore, the player who did it here, hardly needed the help. That season, he stole 38 bases in 43 attempts, a sensational 90 percent.

70: Delayed Triple Steal

Twenty-one years earlier, on October 1, 1987, a *delayed* triple steal occurred in the fourth inning of the Braves–Astros game. With Gerry Perry on third and Ken Oberkfell on second, the Astros intentionally walked Jeff Blauser, loading the bases for Braves pitcher, Jeff Palmer. With Palmer at bat, when the catcher, Ronn Reynolds, threw the ball back to pitcher Danny Darwin, Perry broke for the plate. Aided by Reynolds dropping the return throw, Perry succeeded in stealing home, and the other runners also advanced to complete the triple steal.

COMMENT

Reynolds bruised his hand on the play and was removed from the game—injury added to insult. His replacement, Troy Afenir, immediately allowed another run to score on a passed ball. Undeterred by the chaos, the Astros scored five runs in the seventh and another in the ninth for a walk-off win, despite allowing the Braves seven stolen bases. In less than four innings, Reynolds was "credited" with six steals against and two throwing errors. He had a rough career, batting .188 with four home runs in 356 at-bats spread over six seasons. But Reynolds did enjoy a dose of baseball immortality. In George Plimpton's April Fools article in the 1985 *Sports Illustrated*, Reynolds is the catcher who warms up Sidd Finch and handles his 168-mph fastball.[46]

 # 69: Lightning Strikes Twice

While the two previous plays both featured triple steals, neither was a straight steal with all three runners in motion from the beginning. We know that has happened at least twice because, amazingly, it happened twice *in a single game*. On July 25, 1930, in the first inning the Athletics had Al Simmons on third, Bing Miller on second and Dib Williams on first, with two outs and Jimmy Dykes at bat against the Indians' Pete Appleton. All three runners took off and made it to the next base—a successful triple steal. Just three innings later, against a new pitcher, Milt Shoffner, with two outs the A's again loaded the bases, all Hall of Famers—Mickey Cochrane on third, Al Simmons on second, Jimmy Foxx on first. With Bing Miller batting, the A's again sent all three runners and again all three were safe.

COMMENT

For good measure, Miller proceeded to hit an inside-the-park home run. Cochrane, a Hall of Fame catcher, managed to go 0–6 that game while his teammates racked up 14 runs, but he did steal home. He certainly had a more successful game than his Indians counterpart, Joe Sprinz, who went 0–4 and allowed seven stolen bases.

The second triple steal was particularly audacious, as the A's no longer had the element of surprise on their side. And they sent the runners with two outs, risking taking themselves out of the inning with the bases loaded and a superb batter (Miller) at the plate. The first victimized pitcher, Pete Appleton, was born Pete Jablonowski. He changed his name in 1934, allegedly because the name was too difficult. Bill James proposed a different theory: Jablonowski had recently married Aldora Leszcynski who simply "couldn't stomach the prospect of going through the rest of her life as Aldora Leszcynski Jablonowski."[47]

Milt Shoffner, the other triple steal victim, had a remarkable debut. The 24-year-old, brought up in the middle of the 1929 season, first took the mound on July 20. He was brought in in the seventh inning in the middle of a Yankees rally to face ... Babe Ruth. He struck out Babe. However, Shoffner gave up three runs in the eighth. He ended up kicking around for seven seasons, going 25–26 with an ERA of 4.59. Then again, after fanning the Babe in the clutch, there was nowhere to go but down.

Just as there were two triple steals in one game, there were once two triple-plays in one game. The Twins did the trick against the Red Sox on July 17, 1990. The rally-killers helped the Twins hold the Red Sox to one run (which was unearned). But seeing as it was the only run scored in the game, the Twins managed to lose while making history.

68: Mighty Casey Was Thrown Out

On August 24, 2006, major league baseball witnessed what heretofore had been confined to little league: A player thrown out at first base on an apparent base hit to left field. With the Tigers trailing 7–0 in the fifth inning, Detroit's Sean Casey drilled a ball through the left side of the infield, and White Sox left fielder Pablo Ozuna charged, made a bare-handed pick-up, fired all the way across the diamond, and miraculously nipped Casey at first. Making matters even more embarrassing, Casey bats left-handed. You would think that the extra step closer to first would make the impossible even more impossible (so to speak).

COMMENT

If you're thinking there has to be a catch, you're right—though actually a non-catch. Third baseman Joe Crede lunged for the ball and Casey, mistakenly thinking Crede caught it, started to walk to the dugout. Crede actually did get a piece of leather on the ball, so the play officially goes down as 5–7–3—the only such play in baseball history. There had been other 7–3 putouts, but always left fielders doubling runners off first after a catch. (We saw one such play, with Jim Rice's overthrow of second resulting in an accidental assist at first.)

Casey was indeed ponderous going down the line. He shares (with A.J. Pierzinski) the record for grounding into the most double-plays by a left-handed batter in a season—27 in 2005.

Double-plays is one of those statistics underrated in importance. That season, Casey made 20 more outs than some player with the same on-base percentage. Dick McCauliffe (1967) and Craig Biggio (1997) hit into *zero* double-plays in entire seasons, despite 675 and 744 plate appearances respectively. McCauliffe's achievement is stunning because he was not especially fast: He never stole more than 11 bases in a season, and only eight (while caught seven times) in '67.

On the other hand, McCauliffe struck out 118 times that year. You can't ground into a double-play when you don't make contact. And there is something fluky, or at least random, to these statistics as well. In both the year before and year after Biggio didn't ground into any double-plays, he grounded into ten.

As for Casey, the man who not only grounded into numerous double-plays but managed to get thrown out at first from left-field, you won't guess what he did later in the same game. Yep, he reached on an infield hit.

67: Hitting Outside the Box

As we have seen, home runs have been disallowed for all kinds of reasons. The man who was home run king for 32 years, Henry Aaron, lost one in unique fashion. On August 18, 1965, with the score tied 3–3 in the eighth inning, Cardinals pitcher Curt Simmons tossed a high, loopy change-up—akin to Rip Sewell's famous Eephus pitch or Steve Hamilton's folly floater. Aaron stepped forward and blasted it out of the park, but was called out by umpire Chris Pelekoudas for having left the batter's box when he struck the ball.

COMMENT

The usually mild-mannered Aaron fumed that this was the worst call he had ever seen.[48] He never fully got over it. Bob Uecker, the Cardinals' back-up catcher, reports that Aaron never forgave Uecker for lobbying the ump to make the ridiculous call. But, as Uecker points out (and the box score confirms), the Cards' catcher that day was Tim McCarver.[49] Aaron might have been even more bitter had the Cardinals gone on to win. But in the ninth inning, the Braves' Don Dillard blasted a game-winning homer—his only one of the year (in just 19 at-bats).

Aaron, in addition to his numerous accomplishments, is half of the answer to one of those quirky trivia questions about brother combinations: Which brothers hold the record for most combined home runs? The Aarons, who slugged 768, all but 13 by Hank. Tommie Aaron played parts of seven season with the Braves and hit 13 home runs. Eight were in his rookie year, when Tommie showed potential as a power-speed threat. The eight home runs were in just 334 at-bats (not great but not bad), and he also stole six bases in six attempts.

Thereafter, Tommie managed only five home runs in almost 700 at-bats and three stolen bases in eleven attempts, and was relegated to being half of the answer to a gimmicky trivia question.

Simmons, who served up the negated home run, was not always so lucky. In the best of his 20 seasons, 1950, he helped lead the Whiz Kids Phillies to the World Series. But he couldn't pitch in the fall classic (in which the Phils were swept by the Yankees), because a month earlier he was called to military service during the closing days of the Korean War. And his Phils never again contended. Simmons did get to pitch in a World Series for the Cardinals 14 years later.

66: The Count Is 3 Balls and 0 Pitches

On May 2, 1968, in the seventh inning against the Phillies, Mets shortstop Bud Harrelson stepped up to the plate with a 3–0 count. Huh? Was Harrelson sent in as a pinch-hitter for a batter who somehow got injured taking three pitches? No, the actual explanation is weirder. Harrelson was in the on-deck circle about to step in against the new Phillies' pitcher, John Boozer, when umpire Ed Vargo chose to enforce the new anti-spitball rule penalizing pitchers for going to their mouth while on the mound. That, by rule, meant ball one to the next batter, Harrelson. Philadelphia manager Gene Mauch was so irate that he ordered Boozer to go to his mouth again. Ball two. Wash, rinse, repeat. Ball three. At that point, Vargo ejected both Mauch and Boozer, so the new pitcher, Dick Hall, inherited a 3–0 count.

COMMENT

No problem. Hall got Harrelson to ground out. Boozer's box score for the game? A donut. His name shows up, but 0 innings, 0 hits, 0 walks, 0 strikeouts, 0 runs. Hall, for his part, is one of the greatest athletes you never heard of (unless you happened to be a serious Orioles fan in the 1960s). He was a *five-sport* athlete at Swarthmore—earning all-league honors in football and basketball, dominating in baseball both as a pitcher (career ERA .169) and outfielder (career batting average .412) and I haven't even gotten to his best sport: His 23.25 long jump, in 1951, is still the school record seven decades later. Hall stood 6'6", which helps explain the success in basketball and track.

In the major leagues, Hall is one of the few successful pitchers who was, even if only briefly, a field player. He excelled on the mound, 93–75 with a career ERA of 3.32, and pitched for two World Series champs. In 1964, he was 9–1 for the Orioles, with an ERA of 1.85. Brooks Robinson remembered him as a student of the game with "perfect control." Hall became a full-time pitcher starting 1955. In 1954, he played outfield for the Pirates. He hit just two home runs and batted .239, but was good enough to get in 112 games and come to bat 353 times. And, as far as his overall human talent goes, we shouldn't forget that he graduated from an elite college.

As for Boozer, his teammate Bob Uecker said that Boozer's "idea of fun was to eat bugs and worms and watch people gag."[50] Maybe Gene Mauch knew he was the kind of guy who would not mind baiting an umpire by repeatedly going to his mouth.

65: *Nothing Succeeds Like Failure*

On October 11, 1997, Game 3 of the 1997 ALCS between the Indians and Orioles was tied 1–1 in the bottom of the twelfth inning with the Indians' fleet-footed Marquis Grissom on third base representing the winning run. With Omar Vizquel, a good bunter at the plate, Indians manager, Mike Hargrove, called for a suicide squeeze. As Pitcher Randy Myers went into his delivery, Grissom raced down the line and Visquel squared to bunt. If Vizquel put bat on ball, and nudged the ball into fair territory, the game was over. Of course, if he failed to put bat on ball, Grissom figured to be a dead duck at the plate. (It is called the *suicide* squeeze for a reason.) Nothing went according to plan. Vizquel fanned on his bunt attempt, but catcher Lenny Webster dropped the pitch, allowing Grissom to end the game with a walk-off steal of home on a botched squeeze.

COMMENT

While the Indians celebrated, Orioles manager Davey Johnson stormed onto the field and argued that Visquel fouled off the pitch, which would explain both why Webster missed it and why he retrieved it casually as Grissom scored. In post-game interviews, Webster insisted the ball was fouled whereas Visquel claimed otherwise. Replays were inconclusive.

It was unusual for Vizquel to miss the bunt. Four times he led the

American league in sacrifice bunts, including that season with 16 (and three more in the post-season). Meanwhile, Grissom was particularly grateful for the ending. He had struck out four times in the game and misplayed a fly that allowed the tying run to score. He ended up MVP of the series. Rags to riches.

In a sport full of strange career arcs, Johnson had one of the strangest. Before becoming a successful manager, he enjoyed a 13-year career as a second baseman. In his first seven seasons, he averaged nine home runs per season, normal for a middle infielder in his era. His best year was 1971, when he slugged 18, eight more than his previous high. The next year he hit just five, his lowest output. Displeased by this regression, the Orioles traded Johnson to the Braves. So what happened in 1973—back to his usual seven to ten homers? Not quite. Johnson slugged 43. The tempting explanation is that Johnson benefited enormously from Atlanta's hitter-friendly ballpark. However, he hit 17 of his round-trippers on the road, an impressive home run per 17 at bats. Had the 30-year-old Johnson found power thanks to natural growth, a new hitting coach, or some adjustment at the plate? If so, he lost it just as quickly. The following season, he hit just 15 home runs, and in his remaining years, never more than eight. If this was the 1990s, one would assume that Johnson's 43 home run explosion was abetted by performance-enhancing drugs. Since it was 1973, we can only scratch our heads and marvel that baseball, far more than other sports, experiences such wild outlier seasons.

64: Giant B(r)ummer

On August 22, 1982, the Cardinals and Giants were tied 4–4 in the bottom of the twelfth. The Cardinals loaded the bases with two outs. Glenn Brummer stood at third, the potential winning run. David Green batted, and the count reached 2–2. As the Giants' left-handed pitcher, Gary Lavelle, began his motion, Brummer shocked everyone by taking off, and his head-first slide beat the tag of catcher Milt May for the walk-off stolen base win.

COMMENT

This play is similar to the previous play, but gets the nod for two reasons. First, it was a straight steal of home (a rarity in modern baseball), not a suicide squeeze. Second, the man who stole home for the walk-off victory was not a speedy outfielder but a back-up catcher who stole just four bases in his career. Maybe Whitey Herzog had super powers: He had inserted Brummer into the game as a pinch-runner!

What makes Brummer's steal ridiculously audacious was the two strikes on Green. What happens if Lavelle throws a strike? Green has to let it go and strike out or take a swing and risk beheading Brummer. As it happens, the pitch did appear to be a strike and Green did let it go. Possibly distracted by the runner coming down the line, and out of position because he stepped aside to get a view of the play at the plate, home plate umpire Dave Pallone called it ball three, before calling Brummer safe to end the game. Frank Robinson, the Giants' manager, argued vociferously that the climactic pitch was in fact strike three.

This was hardly the biggest controversy of Pallone's career. In 1988, he was fired after reports of his involvement in a teen sex ring. Charges were later dismissed, and it appears that Pallone's real sin was being outed as gay. A different era. And speaking of changing times, note that the walk-off steal of home used to be reasonably common—it has happened 35 times. But Marquis Grissom's, in the 1997 ALCS, was the last. Most of the 35 were less dramatic than the two that made our list. In most of the walk-off thefts of the plate, the runner stole home as part of a double steal. It is far less remarkable that a runner makes it home when the catcher throws to second. Moreover, Grissom's theft of the plate occurred in a post-season game and required a catcher's muff. Brummer's was a straight steal of home by a notoriously slow runner with two strikes on the batter.

63: To Cap It Off

In the fourth inning of a Mets–Cubs game on September 26, 1979, Cubs outfielder Larry Biittner's cap flew off when he made a diving attempt to catch a line drive off the bat of Bruce Boisclair. Unbeknownst to Biittner, the ball got lodged under the cap. Biittner searched frantically for the ball while Boisclair circled the bases. However, Biittner located the ball under his cap just in time to nail Boisclair at third. Yet another variation on the hidden ball trick.

COMMENT

While not the only player ever with the "double i" in his name (there's also Torii Hunter), Biittner is one of the few with consecutive double letters (double i, double t). Another is Greg Goossen who, despite his unspectacular career, has become part of baseball lore. Casey Stengel allegedly said about him, "I've got a kid here named Goossen. He's 19 years old and in ten years he has a chance to be 29." (Goossen fulfilled Casey's prediction, but was out of baseball by 25.) And in *Ball Four*, Jim Bouton credits Goossen with an observation for the ages. Upon seeing a huge building with a plaque on the front announcing that it had been erected in 1929, Goossen says, "That's quite an erection."[51] Maybe it was that quote that brought Goossen to the attention of actor Gene Hackman. Somehow the two became friends, and Goossen appeared briefly in 15 Hackman movies.

Another double double in the name department is Harry Eells. Pitcher Jimmy Abbott managed a triple double of sorts, though that's cheating because he went by James. Punny department of all's well that ends well, Ewell Blackwell is the only all-star to have "well" in both his first and last names. Blackwell almost made history in more impressive fashion. Baseball devotees know that Johnny Vander Meer is the only pitcher to hurl back to back no-hitters, a feat he accomplished in 1938. Few people know that, nine years later, the side-armed throwing Blackwell (now Vander Meer's teammate) came within two outs of duplicating the feat. A broken bat single by Eddie Stanky went through Blackwell's legs with one out in the ninth inning of the second game.

Fifteen years *before* Vander Meer pulled off the back-to-back no-nos, the feat was almost accomplished by Howard Ehmke. Ehmke achieved fame as the aged journeyman whom Connie Mack mysteriously tapped to pitch Game 1 of the 1929 World Series. All he did was pitch a complete game victory and strike out 13 Cubs. Six years earlier, then with the Red Sox, Ehmke just missed doing something that would have been equally memorable. On September 7, 1923, he pitched a no-hitter against the Philadelphia Athletics. On September 11, he yielded a bad-hop single to the leadoff hitter, Whitey Whit, then set down 27 straight Yankees. Since Whit's base hit bounced off the chest of third-baseman Howard Shanks, an effort was made (supported by an affidavit by the third-base umpire) to get league president Ban Johnson to overturn the official scorer's ruling. Johnson declined. No surprise. This was, after all, year five of the Red Sox curse.

62: Swing and a MISS

On September 27, 1992, Toronto led the Yankees 9–0 when the Jays' Alfredo Griffin led off the top of the fifth against Greg Cadaret. With two strikes, a pitch got away from Cadaret and I mean got AWAY—five feet over the head of catcher Matt Nokes, and way outside to boot. Griffin swung. Not only that, he swung waist-high, missing the pitch by orders of magnitude more than any other batter has ever missed a pitch.

COMMENT

I know what you're thinking: It was a heady play by Griffin, who could now reach first based on the missed strike three. Except Griffin didn't budge, allowing Nokes to retrieve the ball near the backstop and throw to first for the out. What was going on? It had started to rain, the game was not yet official, and with his team up 9–0, Griffin wanted to move things along. The Yankees had other ideas. Billy Martin immediately removed Cadaret. Because Cadaret had just missed the strike zone by 10 feet? More likely a stalling tactic in the hope the rain would pick up. But the Gods mock those who plan. The gamesmanship by both teams was all for naught. The rain stopped and the game went the full nine innings (with the Jays winning 12–2 and Jack Morris notching his 20th win).

The rain-related plotting evokes Norman Rockwell's famous painting, "Bottom of the Sixth," that hangs at the Hall of Fame in Cooperstown. In the painting, during a rain delay, while the umps look at the sky deciding whether the game can resume, Brooklyn's manager needles Pittsburgh's manager, presumably because the inclement weather will prevent the game's completion. The painting seems to miss the boat: The scoreboard shows the score to be 1–0, in Pittsburgh's favor, in the bottom of the sixth. That means the game is official, in which case the wrong manager is mocking his counterpart. Perhaps the Brooklyn manager, who points at the sky, is not indicating inclement weather but rather the fact that the storm is passing. On this reading, he is basically saying: "You thought you'd get a cheap win, but not so fast."

61: Path of No Resistance

Believe it or not, something similar to the previous play happened 77 years earlier. But instead of a mere strikeout, it resulted in what, at least on paper, looks like an accomplishment for the ages. Like most pitchers, Red Faber almost never stole a base: just seven in his twenty-year career. But he stole *three in a single inning.* That's right, he did what Ty Cobb and Rickey Henderson never did, stealing second, third, and home in one go-round.

The date was July 14, 1915. With Faber's White Sox leading the A's in the fourth inning but rain threatening, Faber on first base took a ridiculously large lead, begging the A's to pick him off. (If he wanted to get picked off, what was he doing on base in the first place? It wasn't voluntary. He was hit by a pitch.) When the A's, hoping for the rainout, declined the invitation, Faber stole second. This is easy, he must have thought, and proceeded to steal third. Then came the no-risk steal of home. If they threw him out, great—move the game along and beat the rain. If not, he'd add a run for his team (in case the weather cleared up) and make the record books. The A's allowed him to complete the trifecta.

COMMENT

The pitcher who watched Faber march around the bases was "Bullet" Joe Bush, a colorful character who pitched in 488 games over 17 seasons—none more remarkable than consecutive days in 1916. On August 25, the Indians rocked Bush for five runs in three innings, sending him to his 20th defeat on the season. He was so distraught that he convinced manager Connie Mack to start him the next day. Pitching on zero days rest, Bush walked the leadoff man, Jack Graney, then set down 27 consecutive Indian batters for a no-hitter and near-perfect game.

Just as in the previous play on our list, Alfredo Griffin's deliberate strikeout, Bush's and the A's effort to conspire with Mother Nature proved fruitless: The game went the full nine innings and the A's lost 6–4. The run they gifted Faber and the White Sox proved to be the winning run.

Obviously rainouts and rain-shortened official games have caused many a team a painful loss or non-win. Even a rain delay, without any shortening or cancellation, can cause a team grief. Perhaps the most agonizing rain-affected ballgame was Mets–Padres on July 30, 2015. The Mets led 7–5 in the top of the ninth and, with a hard rain coming down, closer Jeurys Familia recorded two quick outs and a strike on Derek Norris. But when the rain intensified, the umpiring crew called for a delay that lasted 45 minutes. When the rain subsided and the game resumed, Familia returned to the mound, but had lost the edge. Norris singled, so did Matt Kemp, and Justin Upton slugged a three-run home run to put the Padres up 8–7. Now the skies opened up again, causing the umpires to delay the game again.

This time, the Mets hoped the game would be called off, in which case the score would revert to that of the previous inning, and the Mets would win 7–5. It looked like that might happen, as the delay lasted long into the night. But the patient umpires waited until the rain finally let up, and after a two hours and 52 minute delay, the Mets went down quietly in their half of the ninth, leaving them to curse Mother Nature.

60: Round the Merry-Go-Round

On June 21, 2014, in the third inning at Coors field, the Brewers had the bases loaded. Christian Friedrich's pitch got past Rockies catcher Michael McKenry, whose stab at the ball deflected it off the chest protector of the home plate umpire. The ball headed down the first base line, pursued by a scrambling McKenry. The runner on third, Aramis Ramirez, charged home, and McKenry's wild throw got past Friedrich and headed toward the Brewers' dugout. As Friedrich chased it down, Mark Reynolds came around from second for another run. Jean Segura, who began the play at first, decided that *he* could score as well and caught the Rockies by surprise. When Friedrich looked up and saw Segura streaking home, he seemed confused and decided not to throw the ball to McKenry, who had made his way back to the plate. Instead, Friedrich got in a foot race with Segura, but his diving tag came too late. Thus a wild pitch cleared the bases, scoring *three* runs.

COMMENT

Three years earlier, McKenry was on the short end of arguably the worst call in baseball history. On July 26, 2011, his Pirates were in the field in the bottom of the 19th inning against the Braves. With runners on the corners, Scott Proctor's ground ball was snagged by third baseman Pedro Alvarez. Alvarez threw home to McKenry well before the runner, Julio Lugo, arrived. McKenry blocked the plate and tagged Lugo—easy out. Home plate umpire Jerry Meals mysteriously called Lugo safe, ending the game. This call was so bad that one almost suspects that Meals (who received death threats after this game) was dying to go home. The game clocked in at six hours, 39 minutes.

It was an eventful game for McKenry, who homered in the first inning six hours earlier, committed an error, and was caught trying to steal home to win the game in the ninth inning. Needless to say, it was not a straight steal: The runner on first, Brandon Wood, took off and McKenry broke home when the Braves threw to second. Still, why run that play with a slow-footed catcher on third? Well, the pitcher was Craig Kimbrel, nearly unhittable back then, so the Bucs were trying to manufacture a run. Still, it was an odd choice—McKenry's only stolen base attempt of the year. It would be three more years before he would attempt another. It wasn't until his fifth attempt, in his sixth year in the big leagues, that McKenry ever did steal a base.

59: Ball on the Loose

Amazingly, the previous play was not the only time in modern baseball history that three runners scored without the ball being put in play. On June 29, 2001, with the score tied 6–6 in the seventh inning and the bases loaded, the A's Mike Magnante threw a pitch three feet outside that skipped to the backstop. It bounced back to catcher Ramon Hernandez fast enough that he had a play at home on the Rangers' Rafael Palmeiro. Hernandez threw to Magnante covering, but the throw hit Palmeiro on the leg and bounced all the way into the Texas dugout, allowing Ruben Sierra and Gape Kapler to score.

COMMENT

Sierra did well on the base-paths here, but in another play on the 150 Most Bizarre Plays list (spoiler alert: it's top 10) he was guilty of what announcer Jon Miller called (in real time) the worst base-running in baseball history. He was also involved in Play # 58, immediately below, again not running too shrewdly. Kapler, for his part, once tore his Achilles while rounding the bases on a teammate's home run.

Oh, and the winning pitcher in the game who benefited from the A's implosion? Pat Mahomes, Sr. Mahomes won 42 games in his career, and one year went 8–0 for the Mets, but it is safe to say that he does not have the best arm in his family.

58: Wright and Wrong

On April 14, 2002, in the fourth inning the Mariners' Ron Wright batted with first and third, nobody out, against Texas' Kenny Rogers. Wright tapped a bouncer back to Rogers, who threw to shortstop Alex Rodriguez for the force at second. A-Rod threw home way ahead of the base runner Ruben Sierra, who applied the breaks and got in a rundown. Third baseman Hank Blalock tagged Sierra out. Wright tried to take advantage and scamper to second, but Blalock's throw beat him easily. (Pitcher Rogers received the throw by the second base bag. It is hard to say what he was doing there.) Now Wright stopped and created another rundown. Eventually second baseman Michael Young tagged him out for the 1–6–2–5–1–4 triple play.

COMMENT

While this was not the strangest triple-play of all-time (that's coming quite a bit later), it is extra notable because the batter, Ron Wright, was appearing in his first major league game. The triple-play marked his second at-bat. In his first, he struck out with two runners on. In his third and final at-bat, he grounded into a double play. He came up again in the eighth, with the score tied at 7 and a chance for redemption. Except manager Lou Piniella mercifully sent up a pinch-hitter. It was quite a debut for Wright—0–3, making six outs. But here is the really sad part: It was the only game Wright ever played in the major leagues. (Sierra, whose shaky base-running helped Wright make history, otherwise had a pretty good game: 5–5.)

The Braves' Leo Foster had a strikingly similar debut to Wright's, on July 9, 1971. In three at-bats, he flied out, hit into a double-play and triple-play. But Foster at least stuck around for a few seasons and eventually got some base hits.

Believe it or not, Wright is not the only player to hit into a triple-play in his only game. On September 5, 1901, Giants pitcher Larry Hesterfer did the same thing. Yet neither Wright, Foster, nor Hesterfer experienced the worst debut in baseball history. On August 16, 2020, Roel Ramirez, after seven years of toiling in the minors, came on to pitch for the Cardinals in the fifth inning against the White Sox. He inherited a 1–0 deficit, and proceeded to strike out the first batter he faced. But two singles and a walk later, Ramirez faced Yoan Moncada and allowed a grand slam. The next batter, Yasmani Grandal, homered as well. Ditto the next two batters, Jose Abreu and Eloy Jimenez. Having yielded six runs on six hits in two-thirds of an inning, and four consecutive home runs, Ramirez was removed—with an ERA of 81. A few weeks later, without having pitched again, he was sent back to the minors. Thus at least as of this writing, Ramirez's nightmarish debut, like that of Ron Wright, constitutes his entire major league career.

57: Another Tri-Killing

Almost eleven years to the day of the Rangers' triple-play, the Yankees pulled a unique triple-play of their own. Their tri-killing against the Orioles in the eighth inning on April 12, 2013, also started with a ground ball, also involved two rundowns, and also produced a unique scoring—4–6–5–6–5–3–4. The Orioles, down 5–2 at the time, had high hopes when their first two batters reached and Manny Machado came to the plate representing the tying run. One pitch later, the eighth inning was over and the Yankees were three Mariano Rivera outs away from a pre-ordained victory.

COMMENT

The beneficiary of the tri-killing, C.C. Sabathia, was no stranger to this sort of thing. The following April, the Yankees pulled another triple-play with Sabathia on the mound. Four years earlier, in 2010, Sabathia was the beneficiary of still another triple play.

A triple-play enabled Giants reliever, Keiichu Yabu, to pitch the best inning in baseball history. On May 30, 2008, he entered the game against the Padres with the scored tied at 3, runners on first and second, nobody out. Kevin Kouzmanoff swung at Yabu's first pitch and grounded into a triple play—one pitch and three outs for Yabu. He also pitched a perfect ninth and tenth innings, thus facing seven batters and recording nine outs. Kouzmanoff, who we encountered earlier mashing a grand slam in his first MLB at-bat, fared less well in this game: He made nine outs, going 0–6 and hitting into a double-play as well as the triple-play. For good measure, with the score still tied in the 13th inning, Kouzmanoff popped up with the bases loaded. (The Padres withstood his efforts and won the game.)

56: Know When to Fold 'Em

On May 9, 1997, trailing 3–0 in the sixth inning against the Yankees, the Royals loaded the bases with one out against Kenny Rogers. Jeff King grounded to third baseman Charlie Hayes, who stepped on the bag to force out Jose Offerman. Hayes' throw to first, however, was wild, allowing a run to score. Jay Bell, who started the play on first, now streaked past third and towards home. In the process, he raced past Offerman, who was hanging out near third after being forced out. Third base umpire Dale Ford called Bell out for passing Offerman, thereby completing the double-play and ending the inning. Play briefly continued anyway. Rogers ran Bell back toward third and threw to Hayes who, because he knew the inning was over, didn't bother tagging Bell.

The Yankees had already left the field when Crew Chief Rich Garcia overruled Ford's call for the logical reason that you cannot be called out for passing a runner who was already out. The umpires returned Bell to third, King to second, and the Yankees to the diamond.

COMMENT

Naturally Chili Davis then stroked a base hit driving in Bell and King, and the Royals went on to win 7–5. The Yankees protested the game, and had a reasonable argument: Had Ford not made the wrongheaded call that Bell was out for passing Offerman, they had Bell out at third anyway. Hayes would have tagged Bell but for the mistaken call. As Joe Torre lamented post-game: "For an umpire to call out a runner who was not running and then penalize us was bizarre. I can't see how an umpire can stop a play and we get penalized."[52] But Garcia's explanation prevailed: "Once an umpire kills a play like that, what can you do? ... You can't assume the guy was going to be out or score.... There's nothing in the rulebook concerning the play, and we've got to use our judgment."[53] True enough, the rulebook does not address "umpire error."

Torre was less upset by an error Garcia made nine months earlier, when the umpire's mistake helped the Yankees win the ALCS over Baltimore. Garcia ruled a Derek Jeter fly-ball a home run, when the correct ruling would have been fan interference. Twelve-year-old Jeffrey Maier reached over the fence and deflected the ball. Maier became somewhat of a celebrity in New York, and years later a star ballplayer at Wesleyan University.

55: Off the Wall

On July 4, 1934, in the first inning, six of the first eight Phillies reached base, plating three runs off pitcher Walter Beck (who came into the game with a record of 0–4). Dodgers manager Casey Stengel came to the mound to remove his hapless hurler. Beck protested that he should be allowed to stay in, but Stengel demanded the ball. In disgust, Beck turned to the outfield and flung the ball as far as he could. The ball smashed against the right field wall, arousing the Dodgers' right fielder, Hack Wilson, who was daydreaming (or, some said, hung over), hands on knees, head down, eyes closed. When he heard the crash of ball against wall, Wilson assumed that a Phillies batter had connected, and sprang into action. He raced to retrieve the ball and threw a strike to second base, holding the batter to ... oops, as Wilson discovered to his embarrassment, there was no batter.

COMMENT

From that day on, Beck enjoyed the nickname "Boom-Boom." Walter Boom-Boom Beck exemplifies how much pitching has changed. It is no secret that pitchers these days rarely finish what they start. In 2019, Shane Bieber and Lucas Giolito tied for the major league lead with three complete games. In the shortened 2020 season, no one had more than two. Boom-Boom Beck, who played for six teams over a 12-year career, had seasons with 12 and 15 complete games, despite a dismal career record of 39–68. Prior to 2020, the dominant Max Scherzer had 365 career starts, exactly 100 more than Beck. Scherzer had 10 complete games compared to Beck's 44. If we dip back in time before Beck, the disparity is amplified. Starting pitchers on the 1904 Red Sox completed 148 out of 154 games. Apparently relief pitchers were so unreliable that pinch-hitting was rarely deemed worth the at-bat.

Have I mentioned how much I enjoy the names and nicknames of old-timers? In the game Boom-Boom Beck threw the ball off the wall, he was relieved by Ownie Carroll. The winning pitcher for the Phillies was Snipe Hansen. The box scores from the old days can resemble a professional wrestling program.

54: No Time to Argue

On April 30, 1949, with the Cubs leading the Cardinals 3–2, pinch-runner Chuck Diering on first and two outs in the ninth inning, the Cards' Rocky Nelson hit a line drive to shallow left. Andy Pafko made a diving catch, sealing the victory for the Cubs. Except umpire Al Barlick ruled that Pafko trapped the ball. Pafko stormed over to Barlick and they went nose to nose while Diering and Nelson circled the bases. At the last second Pafko decided to resume play and threw home, but his throw hit Nelson as he slid in for what would prove to be the game-winning run.

COMMENT

The official scorer called it a home run. Such are the quirks of baseball custom which does not consider most errors of omission, no matter how egregious, to be errors. As for Pafko's egregious (non) error, he must have waged quite an argument with Barlick in order to allow Nelson to make it home. The notoriously slow Nelson managed just seven stolen bases in his long career. For that matter, Diering was a curious choice to pinch-run. He attempted seven steals that year and succeeded only once. During his nine-year career, he stole 16 bases and was caught 33 times, an abysmal success rate of 31 percent. Then again, everything is a case of compared to what: The man Diering ran for, Eddie Kazak, stole zero bases in his five-year career.

The Cardinals won the game despite their starting pitcher, Cloyd

Baker, lasting just one third of an inning. Baker was the older brother of third basemen Ken and Clete. The three brothers combined for 444 home runs. Cloyd contributed zero, despite 132 plate appearances. But, thanks to him, they are the only brother combination to combine for more than 400 home runs and 20 wins on the mound. Cloyd was 20–23 lifetime.

53: Moon Shot Lands

A similar play happened five years later. On August 13, 1954, with the Cardinals and Reds tied 8–8 in the ninth inning, the bases were loaded with two outs for the Cards' Wally Moon. Moon blasted a ball to left center that Gus Bell caught on his shoestrings—or so it seemed. Third base umpire Babe Pinelli ruled catch, but second base umpire Bill Stewart ruled trap. Two Cardinals scored before the confused Bell threw home in time to nail Joe Frazier. The umpires decided that the call belonged to Stewart, so the two runs counted—giving the Cardinals a 10–8 lead that they held. Superstitious Reds fans will note that the game took place on Friday the 13th.

COMMENT

Reds manager Birdie Tebbetts was so incensed by the call that he got himself ejected. According to newspaper accounts, Tebbets told Stewart: "You're a lousy umpire. You blew it in the World Series. You blew it in the all-star game. Why don't you quit?"[54] Tebbetts was a philosophy major at Providence College, but here logic failed him: If Stewart was a lousy ump, why was he assigned the World Series and All Star game? In fact, in a 22-season career, Stewart worked five World Series and four all-star games and, for good measure, refereed 11 National Hockey League seasons.

The starting pitchers in the Cards–Reds game, Joe Nuxhall and Harvey Haddix, had staggeringly similar careers. Nuxhall was 135–117 with 20 shutouts and 19 saves; Haddix, 136–113, with 20 shutouts, 20 saves. They were both born in Ohio towns less than 60 miles apart.

The Reds inserted Rocky Bridges at the start of the ninth inning— just before everything fell apart. Bridges, a minor-leagues manager after his playing career, achieved some fame when Jim Bouton's book,

I Managed Good but Boy Did they Play Bad, took its title from a quote by Bridges. A lifetime .247 hitter, he nevertheless merited a 1964 *Sports Illustrated* profile devoted to his sense of humor. When he hit his first home run in two years in 1961, Bridges quipped that "I'm still behind Babe Ruth, but I've been sick."[55]

52: *White Heat*

In the same vein as the previous play but even weirder was a play just two years later. On August 28, 1956, with Detroit ahead 3–0 in the sixth inning, and Bill Tuttle on second base, Red Wilson's ground-ball was fielded by Red Sox shortstop Milt Bolling behind second. Tuttle raced home, Bolling threw home, and Sox catcher Sammy White applied the tag, but Tuttle was called safe. This so incensed White that he heaved the ball into center field. Wilson raced home, scoring on a play that started with his groundball to short. Centerfielder Jimmy Piersall retrieved the ball and threw it back to the infield, but the Red Sox infielders were busy watching White berate the umpire, Frank Umont and thus failed to take action.

COMMENT

It is no surprise that Piersall would make numerous appearances in a book about baseball bizarro, but in this instance he was the one player on the field who behaved rationally. White, for his part, was capable of Piersall-like behavior (as his throw into centerfield indicates). On June 11, 1952, he hit a walk-off grand slam off of Satchel Paige. After rounding third, he dropped to the ground, crawled home, and kissed the dish.

The winning pitcher who benefited from White's tantrum, Frank Lary, notched his 14th victory and didn't lose again that season, leading the American League with 21 wins. Lary also led the league in hit batters with 12, a feat he repeated the next two years (both the 12 and leading the league). Then, after one disappointing year (he plunked only 11 and was nosed out for the league lead by Johnny Kuks), in 1960 he again led the league, this time with 19. While most statistics can be misleading, a pitcher's hit batsmen is particularly slippery: It may mean the pitcher has poor control, but it can mean the opposite. Don Drysdale hit 17 batters one year while walking just 45 in 273 innings—an exceptionally low walk total accompanying the exceptionally high total of hit batsmen. Lary, like Drysdale, had good control; they could plunk batters when they wanted to.

Umont, the umpire on the play who so incensed Sammy White, was the first major league umpire to wear glasses. I have a feeling that White and other players let Umont know what they thought that said about his vision.

51: Fire Drill

In the sixth inning against the Mariners on August 22, 2017, the Braves had runners on first and second with one out. Shortstop Jean Segura made a diving stop on Ender Inciarte's chopper up the middle, but fumbled the ball, costing him any chance at second or first. Segura wisely pivoted and threw to third-baseman Kyle Seager, catching Ozzie Albies rounding third and forcing him into a run-down. Seager threw to catcher Mike Zunino, but Zunino's return throw squirted off Seager's glove and behind the bag, leading Albies to sprint home. Segura, who started the play near second base, now retrieved the ball behind third and threw to the plate, which was covered by first baseman Yonder Alonso. Albies beat the throw. By now, Braves dotted the diamond—Lane Adams was in no man's land between second and third and Inciarte wandered between first and second. Alonso made a mad dash toward Inciarte. When Inciarte made it safely to second, Alonso threw to Zunino (the catcher now covering third) to catch Adams. The Mariners ran a fire drill (6–5–2–6–3–2) to get one out while allowing a run to score.

COMMENT

This is one of three plays in our 150 involving Segura, one of the few players to achieve that distinction. It is not entirely a coincidence. Every aspect of Segura's game, good and bad, tends toward action: He puts the ball in play (having exceptionally low walk and strikeout rates), attempts to steal a fair amount, and is always among the league-leaders in errors at shortstop. By contrast, Lane Adams, the runner whom the Mariners finally nabbed, is not one from whom you would expect sloppy base-running. In his limited time in the big leagues, Adams has attempted 11 steals and never been caught.

50: Radar Detector Needs Calibration

On May 28, 2019, in the third inning the Rays' Avasail Garcia launched a fly ball to medium right. Blue Jays right fielder Randal Grichuk came in a good ten feet, the situation seemingly under control, until the ball dropped 20 feet behind him. Garcia sprinted round the bases for an inside-the-park home run on a routine fly-ball.

COMMENT

Had Grichuk lost the ball in the lights? Or against the Tropicana Field dome? It doesn't seem so. Jays manager Charlie Montoyo passed along Grichuk's explanation for the mishap: "He said that he got disorientated."[56] (Possibly the same explanation for his aforementioned base-running blunder—see Play # 115.) The Rays won the game 3–1, just missing a shutout by one out—Grichuk scored in the ninth inning. For fans not well-versed in the modern game, it would have been an unrecognizable shutout. Tampa Bay used five pitchers, none of whom lasted four innings. The starter, Ryne Stanek, pitched two scoreless innings. He threw 26 pitches, 25 more than Chaz Roe, who came on in the sixth inning, retired Grichuk on a fly-ball with his first pitch, and retired to the clubhouse for a well-earned shower.

Grichuk's disorientation calls to mind the explanation by quirky Dodgers pitcher Billy Loes for misplaying a groundball in the 1952 World Series: He insisted he lost it in the sun. That same World Series, Loes committed the first balk in World Series history, when the ball fell from his hand as he started his windup. He had an interesting explanation for that one too: "Too much spit on it."[57] Loes' best-known utterance was that he did not want to win 20 games because "then I'd be expected to do it every year."

49: Wacky Walk-Off

In the bottom of the eleventh inning against the A's on July 10, 2018, the Astros had the winning run on second with two outs when Alex Bregman tapped a ball in front of the plate for the easiest out imaginable. Catcher Jonathan Lucroy simply had to tag Bregman, who had barely left the batter's box. But when Lucroy went to do so, Bregman pulled back like Muhammad Ali eluding a punch with lightning-fast reflexes. Still, no problem, because Lucroy stood between Bregman and first base. However, when Lucroy went to apply the tag again, he slipped, and Bregman eluded him again, and headed down the baseline. To make matters worse for Lucroy, as he stumbled he dropped the ball. As if that weren't bad enough, the ball brushed against the umpire's body, slightly altering its course. Despite the difficulties, Lucroy picked up the ball and fired to first in plenty of time. Except his throw caromed off Bregman's helmet and sailed into right-field. Kyle Tucker scampered home for the walk-off win. The A's challenged the play, presumably on the theory that no team should have to lose on a play like that.

COMMENT

Bregman slugged two homers on the day, but his game-winning at-bat involved a ball that travelled two feet. Seven years earlier, Lucroy was involved on the positive side of another unusual walk-off: On May 28, 2011, his suicide squeeze with the bases loaded brought home Ryan Braun and lifted the Brewers to a 3–2 win over the Giants. The suicide squeeze is almost impossible to defend against, which raises an obvious question: Why isn't it used more often? A great question with no obvious answer.

48: Herd of Birds Lift Indians

On June 11, 2009, in the bottom of the tenth inning of a tie game between the Indians and Royals, with the Tribe's Shin-Soo Choo at the plate and Mark DeRosa the potential winning run on second, a few dozen seagulls camped out in center field surrounding the Royals' CoCo Crisp. In retrospect, Crisp probably should have requested a timeout while something was done to disperse the intruders. Lo and behold, Choo hit a line drive base hit to center. Crisp charged, and probably could have held DeRosa at third had the seagulls not swarmed around him and made it impossible for him to locate the ball. It whipped past him, and DeRosa scored the winning run.

COMMENT

We have heard of balls lost in the sun or the lights but lost in the seagulls? If birds can affect a ballgame, how about insects? Game 2 of the 2007 ALDS between the Yankees and Indians turned on a swarm of insects that chose for refuge the neck of Yankees pitcher Joba Chamberlain. The rookie had been unhittable since joining the club in August, so the Yankees felt good about their chances when he started the eighth inning protecting a one-run lead, with Mariano Rivera poised to pitch the ninth. But the insects undid Chamberlain (two walks, two wild pitches, and a hit batter) despite repeated sprayings of insecticide from the team trainer. The Indians tied the score and went on to win the game and series.

Non-human creatures interfering with the game tees up another Babe Ruth story, one that would easily make our list of bizarre plays if it could be verified. It has been widely reported that when a dog wandered onto the field at Comiskey Park, Babe threw his mitt at it and the dog ran off with the mitt. Sure, enough, the batter lofted a fly ball to left that Babe speared with his bare hands.

Unlike many urban legends, this one comes with substantial details. One reads in several places that the play occurred on August 20, 1923, the player who hit the ball was Paul Castner, and at the time the Yankees led 16–5 in the ninth. The box score for that game confirms several of these facts: The Yankees did defeat the White Sox by that score, and Castner did fly out to Ruth in the ninth inning. Needless to say, the play-by-play accompanying the box score does not specify whether the catch was barehanded (or, for that matter, whether a dog was running around the outfield). But if someone fabricated the dog and the bare-hand catch, they went to the trouble of finding an actual game to graft their imagination onto. Perhaps the story has an element of truth but is embellished. It would seem that newspaper accounts of the game would settle it, insofar as dog-steals-mitt would surely become part of any such account. No newspaper account of the game mentions the dog and bare-hand catch.

You could write an entire book about the most bizarre plays that never happened but are nevertheless part of baseball lore. Consider a legendary play by the notoriously poor outfielder, Smead Jolley. Jolley was so poor defensively that he lasted only four years in the big leagues despite a lifetime batting average of .305 and pretty good power. Allegedly, in a game in September 1931, Bing Miller smacked a single that went through Jolley's legs. Jolley turned around in time to play the carom off the wall, but it went through his legs again! Undaunted, he retrieved the ball and threw to third to try to nail Miller. The ball sailed over the third baseman's head, allowing Miller to score. Alas, the play did not happen. Jolly never committed two errors on a single play, much less three.

47: Good News, Bad News

On April 12, 1987, in the third inning against the defending World Champion Mets, Atlanta's Dion James hit a routine fly-ball to the out-field that struck a pigeon mid-air, and fell (both ball and bird) to Earth for a double.

COMMENT

The play shows up in the Dowd Report that led to Pete Rose's banishment from baseball. Partly because of the pigeon. James came around to score on Dale Murphy's home run, which helped lift the Braves to a victory that cost Rose $4,800—his single biggest bet. The play was a good reminder that no one should bet on baseball, not just managers. How can you account for things like avian interven-tion? In this case, the Braves did not need the help. They scored seven runs in the seventh inning to win 12–4. In the lucky seventh, the first eight Braves to bat reached based. But that didn't exactly threaten the record—the 1952 Dodgers once had *19* consecutive batters reach base. The magic number that day was 19, as the Dodgers won 19–1. Surprisingly, only one Dodger had more than two hits on the day— the pitcher, Chris Van Cuyk, who went 4–5 to go along with pitch-ing a complete game. Three months after his dream game, Van Cuyk was out of the big leagues for good, having won just seven games in his career.

46: Warning Track Power

On April 9, 2019, at Busch Stadium, in the eighth inning with the Dodgers trailing the Cardinals 4–0, Cards left fielder Marcell Ozuna leaped atop and draped himself on the wall, setting himself up to attempt a spectacular catch on the fly ball off the bat of Enrique Her-nandez. Unfortunately for Ozuna, the ball landed in the middle of the warning track. As Ozuna realized how badly he had misjudged the ball, and tried to return to terra firma to make the play, his feet got tangled and he fell flat on his face on the warning track. Lucky for him, the ball hopped the fence for a ground-rule double rather than staying in play for an even more embarrassing triple or inside-the-park home run.

COMMENT

Ever wonder about the arbitrary nature of official scoring? Ozuna committed a pair of obvious blunders—a double baseball blooper in a single play. True disaster, yet he was charged with *no* error. Whereas an outfielder can make a perfect throw home, be about to receive an assist and ovation, when the ball hits a pebble and takes a bad hop over the catcher's head—if any runners advance, he is charged with an error. For a perfect throw.

Errors contribute to the arbitrariness of other statistics. Does it make sense to reconstruct how an inning would have developed without the error in order to determine how many earned runs to charge a pitcher? In fact, ERA is unwieldy all around. Consider a scenario where Pitchers A and B both experience an error behind them with two outs. Pitcher A calmly gets the third out, whereas Pitcher B implodes, allows eight straight hits and seven runs. Neither gets charged with an earned run: As far as their ERAs are concerned, they were equally effective. But perhaps the single oddest feature of baseball statistics is the definition of a pitcher's WHIP: walks plus hits per inning pitched. Sounds reasonable, right? It gauges how effective a pitcher is at keeping runners off base. Except for one quirk: WHIP does not include batters hit by pitch. Why in the world not? The only explanation I can think of is that the neat acronym WHIP would not be usable if a new element was added. Talk about the tail wagging the dog.

Speaking of both misleading statistics and shaky official scoring customs, how about the rule requiring the starting pitcher to complete five innings to be eligible for the win? The Cardinals survived Ozuna's face plant and won the game 4–0. The starter, Dakota Hudson, pitched four and two-thirds innings of shutout ball—not enough to pick up the win, even though the Cardinals led 3–0 when he departed and never relinquished the lead. Instead, the win went to John Brebbia, who retired just four batters.

45: He Said "Please"

On August 7, 1915, in the seventh inning against the Dodgers, with the score tied 4–4, the Cardinals had a runner on third and two outs against rookie pitcher Ed Appleton. The Cardinals' third base coach, Miller Huggins, asked Appleton to toss him the ball to inspect it. He must have asked politely, because Appleton obliged. Huggins stepped aside and let the ball roll away, as Dots Miller raced home.

COMMENT

The wily Huggins, later the manager of the dominant Yankees teams of the 1920s and elected to the Hall of Fame in 1964, is also widely credited with having invented the delayed steal. Though he was the Yankees manager at the time, Huggins was not responsible for the most ill-fated attempted steal in baseball history: Babe Ruth getting thrown out to end the 1926 World Series with the Yankees trailing by one run. While this has been widely proclaimed a blunder, Ruth explained that he made the attempt (on his own) for two reasons: Pitcher Grover Cleveland Alexander was paying no attention to him and, with Alexander (having come on in relief in the eighth) throwing darts, Ruth did not believe the Yankees could string together multiple hits. Two pretty good reasons, though it needs to be added that Ruth was not a good base stealer. On his career, He stole 127 bases in 246 attempts (post-season included), a mediocre 52 percent clip.

As for Huggins' brilliant coaching move at the expense of poor Ed Appleton, it raises this question: If that was the best third-base coaching of all time, what is the worst? A great candidate is a play attributed to one George Smith, Brooklyn's third-base coach, in a game in 1890. Allegedly, caught up in the excitement of waving a runner home, Smith accompanied the runner all the way down the baseline. The confused catcher tagged Smith instead of the base runner. After a prolonged argument, the umpires ruled the runner out based on coach's interference. In 1904, the rulebook was amended specifically to prohibit coach's interference.

On at least one occasion, this rule decided a game. On September 5, 2010, the Tigers left the tying run on third in the ninth inning of a 6–5 loss to the Twins. The final out came when third-base coach Dave Anderson was called for interference for touching hands with Michael

Young to help stop Young's race to the plate and return him to the bag. Less than a year later, on August 4, 2011, the Orioles lost 3–2 to the Rays with the help of coach's interference. With one out in the seventh inning, the Orioles had runners on second and third when Chris Richard scorched a base hit to center. As Brady Anderson dashed around third, coach Tom Trebelhorn threw up the stop sign. But he got a little too close: Anderson plowed into Trebelhorn and the two got tangled up. Umpire John Hirschbeck called Anderson out on account of Trebelhorn's interference.

44: Pick Up the Ball!

In a spring training game on March 24, 2016, in the second inning against the Mets, the Astros' AJ Reed blasted a shot to Tradition Field's centerfield wall that seemed to get stuck between the fence's padding and the ground. Mets centerfielder Yoenis Céspedes stopped running, so Reed did the same, pulling into second base with the ground-rule double. But when the Astros' bench screamed at Reed to resume running, he did so, and crossed home plate while the ball sat harmlessly under the wall and Céspedes remained a spectator. Second-base umpire C.B. Bucknor jogged out to examine the evidence. He and Céspedes discussed the matter briefly, and then Bucknor spread his arms in the safe sign—home run. To prove the point, Bucknor bent over and swatted the ball a few feet away. It simply wasn't lodged into the padding. What was Céspedes thinking?

COMMENT

Absent a miracle, like Céspedes' cooperation, Reed could never hit an inside-the-park home run. In four years in the major leagues, he has zero triples and zero steals. In fact, he has zero steal *attempts*. Russ Nixon played in 906 games spanning 13 seasons without a successful steal, but he at least tried (seven times). Gus Triandos also lasted 13 years, but played in 300 more games than Nixon, and attempted exactly one steal. He was successful.

As for Céspedes, he struggled with inside-the-parkers. On the first pitch of the 2015 World Series, Kansas City's Alcides Escobar lofted a shot to left center that Céspedes should have caught. But he failed to get his glove up and the ball hit his foot and careened into left-field, while Escobar circled the bases for the first World Series inside-the-park home run in 86 years (and perhaps the only first-pitch-of-the-game inside-the-park home run ever).

43: Non-Ivy League Move

In a remarkably similar play to Céspedes's blunder, in the fourth inning at Wrigley Field on June 29, 2004, Cubs left fielder Moises Alou caught up to a base hit by Houston's Adam Everett that rolled toward the wall, then deliberately slapped the ball into the ivy with his glove, and screamed for a ground-rule double. The umpires ignored Alou's silliness, and Everett raced all the way home.

COMMENT

This time the official scorer credited Everett with a double and charged Alou with a two-base error. Evidently Alou slapping the ball made this an error of commission and not a mere error of omission.

Alou displayed equally bizarre and more consequential behavior the previous year, when his tantrum over being interfered with by a fan encouraged Cub fans to blame the fan, Steve Bartman, for the team's NLCS defeat. Poor Bartman was driven into hiding. Much of the media and many fans bought into the absurd idea that a fan in the stands cost the Cubs the series. Bartman did what fans have always done, going for a souvenir on a foul ball in the stands.

Alou was a character. One of the few players not to use batting gloves, he would instead urinate on his hands to toughen them up.

#42: In the Cheap Seats

Our bizarre plays have featured an inside-the-park home run when an outfielder toppled into the seats, and another when the ball stopped under the fence. Hunter Pence, then with the Rangers, hit an inside-the-parker that combined these improbable features. On June 11, 2019, at Fenway Park, in the sixth inning the Red Sox's right fielder, Brock Holt, lunged to try to catch Pence's fly to deep right and fell partway into the bleachers. With Holt out of commission, the ball rolled along the right-field wall until it settled under the wall. Pence could have walked around the bases twice.

COMMENT

The game marked the first career start for Red Sox pitcher Darwinzon Hernandez, a notably strange debut. Hernandez struck out the side in the first inning, but lasted only two batters into the fourth. In the first three innings, he struck out or walked 12 of the 16 batters he faced (seven strike outs, five walks). Exceptionally unusual, but not for Hernandez. On the season, he averaged one walk and two strikeouts per inning.

Killer trivia question: Who are the only two players ever to hit two inside-the-park home runs in a single game? Dick Allen and Greg Gagne.

41: We'll Meet Again

On July 11, 1963, in the top of the second inning, on a hit and run, Willie Mays raced for second while Orlando Cepeda tapped a ground ball to Phillies second baseman Tony Taylor. Mays never broke stride rounding second, figuring he could make it to third by the time the Phils completed two throws. But Taylor read Mays' mind and never threw to first. Instead, he threw to third, where he had Mays by a mile. Mays turned back toward second, chased by the third baseman, Don Hoak, while Cepeda raced toward second from the opposite direction. Cepeda and Mays arrived together. Two players occupying a base simultaneously is amusing but far from unique. But in this instance Hoak dropped the ball before he could tag Mays and Cepeda. (Infielders in that situation always tag both runners, not taking any chances with respect to who is entitled to the bag.) Hoak's drop gave new life to the play. Mays and Cepeda now each figured he better depart the base and leave it to his teammate—Mays headed back toward third while Cepeda returned to first. Taylor retrieved the ball and, for the second time in a single play, threw to third to trap Mays, who for the second time in a single play got into a rundown between second and third. He was finally tagged out by Taylor, while Cepeda, who had returned safely to first, wisely decided to leave well enough alone and stay there.

COMMENT

Any play involving Mays calls to mind his legendary catch in the 1954 World Series. I hate to say it, especially since it may cause readers to demand my placement in a straitjacket, but the catch is overrated. While Mays traveled a great distance to make a fine play, it was clearly less difficult than the many times Torii Hunter climbed a wall to prevent a home run or Jim Edmonds' uphill, full-out dive in Houston, among numerous other catches over the years.

Indeed, at the time, Mays' catch was not regarded with awe. The *New York Times* next-day story on the game was titled "Giants Win in 10 From Indians 5–2 on Rhodes' Homer." The third subtitle notes "Mays' Catch Saves Triumph," but the actual article does not mention the catch until the 35th paragraph.[58] The *Times* sports section did devote two short articles to the catch, but they belie the notion that it was regarded as *the catch*. One, "Reminder of Gionfriddo," relates Joe DiMaggio's opinion that Al Gionfriddo's catch in the 1947 World Series (robbing DiMaggio) was better than Mays' catch.[59] In the other, "Mays' Catch Appraised," a Giants scout reels off several catches by Mays that he considers better.[60]

Perhaps Mays' catch became mega-hyped because it came in a World Series? Plays become immortalized because of the moment as much as the play itself. But there has never been a shortage of great World Series catches. The 1912 Series featured a pair (one by Fred Snodgrass on the very next play following his immortal muff), including Josh Devore's leaping *bare-hand* catch to end Game 3, with the would-be tying and winning runs heading home. In a single game in the 1952 World Series, the Dodgers' outfield made three sensational plays, two robbing Yankees of home runs. Ron Swoboda's astounding catch in 1969 was in a World Series. Joe Rudi made several sparklers in the 1972–74 World. Devon White made an eye-defying catch in the 1992 World Series when he won a collision with the center field wall. Endy Chavez's wall-climber for the Mets in 2007 was in Game 7 of a League Championship Series, as close to a World Series as you can get.

Still, one must say this for Mays' catch: It gave rise to one of the great lines of all-time, from the Giants' pitcher who benefited from the catch, Don Liddle. Liddle had been called in to face Wertz, who promptly greeted him with the mortar shot run down by Mays. Liddle was immediately removed from the game and blithely observed, "Well, I got my man."[61]

40: Check the Ruhlebook

Game 4 of the 1980 NLCS between the Astros and Phillies, on October 11, 1980, has already made our list of most bizarre plays— see Play # 100. That play occurred in the bottom of the fourth. In the top half, the Phillies had Bake McBride on first and Manny Trillo on second with no outs when Garry Maddox hit a soft line drive at the feet of pitcher Vern Ruhle. Ruhle either caught the ball or trapped it, depending on which umpire you believed: Home plate umpire Doug Harvey signaled no catch but the first and third base umpires signaled catch. Ruhle threw to first baseman Art Howe to either double off Trillo or retire Maddox (depending on whether Maddox's liner was caught or trapped). Meanwhile Trillo had raced to second and McBride to third. Even as the umpires had begun a conference to sort things out, Howe ran over to second to tap the bag for the possible triple-play.

The Astros left the field, convinced they had a triple-play, which they did if Ruhle was deemed to have caught the ball. If he had trapped the ball, then the only out they recorded was at first base and the Phillies had runners on second and third with just one out. After a brief conference, Harvey signaled that Ruhle had indeed caught the ball and the Astros had their inning-ending triple-play. The Phillies instantly swarmed Harvey protesting vehemently, prompting him to hold another conference, this time involving all six umpires. (As this was a post-season game, there were umpires down the outfield lines.) That conference was followed by a meeting between Harvey and National League president Chub Feeney, who was seated in the first row behind home plate. Harvey emerged from all the consultation with a compromise—a double-play.

COMMENT

The umpiring crew did not acknowledge that they deliberately produced a split-the-difference decision. Rather, the men in blue ruled that Ruhle did indeed catch the ball, and his throw to first therefore doubled off Trillo. Why no triple-play? Because McBride had been misled by Harvey's mistaken call of no catch, without which he would not have run to third. (For a different approach to the "deceived by umpire" situation, see Plays # 56 and # 28.)

It is unclear why the umps did not decide that Trillo was also misled. Maybe the theory was that he was closer to the first-base umpire who called the play a catch, and thus had no excuse for leaving the base. Or maybe they felt he could not have gotten back to the base regardless. In any event, the ruling left the Phillies with a runner on second, two out, and neither team the slightest bit happy. Both managers announced that they were playing the game under protest! The Phillies prevailed 5–3, and the Astros' protest was denied.

If you think this play presented a great example of the benefit of replay review, think again. Replays were inconclusive as to whether Ruhle caught or trapped the ball. So, had replay review been available (which it obviously wasn't in 1980), the umps would have had to stick with the original call, which was ... unclear. Different umps called it differently, which was the source of the confusion in the first place.

39: Anarchy

On April 11, 2012, the Rockies, batting against the Giants in the bottom of the fifth inning, had Todd Helton on second and Michael Cuddyer at first when Ramon Hernandez singled to center. Angel Pagan came up throwing while Helton scampered home. First baseman Brett Pill tried to cut off the throw near the mound, but the ball deflected off his glove and rolled over the first base line where catcher Hector Sanchez slid to corral it halfway between home and first. Cuddyer charged home, but Sanchez's throw to pitcher Jeremy Affeldt, covering the plate, had him beat easily. Cuddyer retreated into a rundown. Sanchez threw to third baseman Pablo Sandoval, who chased Cuddyer home. However, when Sandoval tried to flip the ball to Sanchez, who by now had reclaimed the plate, the ball fell out of his hand, allowing Cuddyer to score. Sandoval did not give up. He picked up the ball and fired to third, which was now covered by shortstop Brandon Crawford, to try to catch the advancing Hernandez. Crawford dove, but Hernandez's hook slide eluded him—while also eluding the bag. With both players on the ground, they each dove again (Hernandez in search of the bag and Crawford in search of Hernandez), with Hernandez sneaking in safely.

COMMENT

The seven-run inning helped the Rockies prevail 17–8. The Giants also had a seven-run inning. Both teams scoring a touchdown in an inning is not something that happens every game but, when it does, is likely to be at Coors Field. Three weeks after this one, Affeldt sprained an MCL while picking up his four-year-old son. He missed the last 19 games of 2011 when he cut his hand separating frozen hamburger patties. In 2015, Affeldt landed on the DL with another child-related injury, twisting his knee while playing with his three sons at a lake. None of those qualifies as the strangest baseball injury ever. My vote goes to Yoenis Céspedes suffering a sprained ankle in a fight with a wild boar on his Florida ranch. Runner-up to Trevor Bauer, who had to leave a playoff game because the stitches opened up on the pinkie of his pitching hand: He sliced the finger on the propellers of his drone. Honorable mention to Rickey Henderson, who missed three games from frostbite incurred when he soaked his foot in ice for too long. The winner might be John Smoltz, who allegedly burned himself while ironing a shirt *he was wearing*, but there is no evidence to support that widespread rumor.

38: *Déjà vu All Over Again*

On August 17, 1957, in Philadelphia, Richie Ashburn drilled a line drive into the crowd, striking and breaking the nose of a woman named Alice Roth, wife of the sports editor for a Philadelphia newspaper. A stretcher was summoned to carry Roth off. On the next pitch, Ashburn hit another line drive into the crowd, which hit poor Ms. Roth (lying on the stretcher) on the hip.

COMMENT

Ashburn's "achievement" has not gone unnoticed. The entertaining sportswriter, Jason Stark, noted that "no matter how good Mantle and Mays may have been, they never had a day like Ashburn had on August 17, 1957."[62] Ashburn got two of the Phillies' four hits in a 3–1 win over the Giants, but I'm pretty sure Stark was referring to his double beaning of poor Alice Roth.

Ms. Roth was arguably not the unluckiest spectator ever. On May 14, 1939, in Comiskey Park, Bob Feller pitched in front of a large crowd that included his parents, who made the 250-mile trek from their Iowa home. Early in the game, a foul ball off Feller's fast-ball creamed ... his mother. She had to be taken away, and though she was not seriously injured, she missed most of her son's complete game victory. The really weird thing is that Mrs. Feller's ill-fated visit to the ballpark didn't happen any old day, but rather on Mother's Day. The *really*, *really* weird thing is that this stranger-than-fiction history repeated itself in a spring training game in 2010, when Denard Span's line drive struck his mother just below her collarbone. Spam, realizing what had happened, sprinted to the stands, hopped over the wall, and tended to his mom. After a five-minute delay, he returned to the plate with a 3–2 count and promptly struck out looking.

The incident took place on March 31, which meant it was reported in newspapers around the country on April 1 and surely regarded by many as an April Fool's prank. As they say, you can't make this stuff up.

37: Unprecedented Coaching Move Yields Triple-Play

On July 26, 2015, the Mariners pulled off a 3–6–2–2 triple-play. Incredibly, it was not the first 3–6–2–2 triple play: There was an earlier one in 1955. But the 2015 version was even crazier. In the top of the fourth, the Jays, leading 4–3, had Kevin Pillar on first and Ezequiel Carrera on third with no outs. Ryan Goins laced a groundball to first baseman Mark Trumbo. Trumbo stepped on the bag for the first out. He looked up and saw Carrera hold at third. Pillar, meanwhile, had stopped between first and second. (Trumbo stepping on first eliminated the force at second.) Trumbo wheeled and threw to shortstop Brad Miller. While executing the run-down to try to get Pillar, Miller kept an eye on Carrera who was dancing down the third-base line threatening to run home. Finally Carrera broke home and Miller threw to catcher Mike Zunino, forcing Carrera into a run-down. While Zunino chased Carrera back to third, Pillar sped around second and joined the party at third. With two runners now co-occupying third, Zunino tagged them both to be on the safe (out?) side, though of course Pillar was the only one out. For reasons that remain unknown, third base coach Luis Rivera, who had unsuccessfully implored Pillar to reverse course and retreat to second, now pushed Carrera, as if trying to get him to head home. Thanks to the nudge, Carrera stumbled and lost contact with the bag. Zunino tagged him out for the coach-assisted triple-play.

COMMENT

The play proved critical as the Mariners won the game 6–5 in ten innings. We will never know whether the third-base umpire would have called Carrera out if he kept his foot on the bag. Technically, he should have: Rivera's shove constituted coach's interference. Under Rule 6.01 (a)(8), a runner is out if "in the judgment of the umpire, the base coach at third base, or first base, by touching or holding the runner, physically assists him in returning to or leaving third base or first base." Coach's interference is not novel. (See comment attached to Play # 45.) But a coach knocking his player off the bag to create a triple-play definitely is.

Zunino had quite a game. In addition to making two put-outs on the triple-play, he had three hits and threw out the only runner who attempted to steal. A few weeks later, he was sent to Triple A. And so it goes.

36: Who's on First?

In the third inning of the Tigers–Indians game on May 1, 2009, Detroit's Josh Anderson chopped a grounder to first. Victor Martinez knocked the ball down but it bounded away, near the base-line several feet in front of the bag. Martinez chased it down, arriving at the same time as Anderson. Martinez attempted to scoop the ball and tag Anderson in one motion, and Anderson attempted to leap-frog the tag. Neither fared well. The ball squirted out of Martinez's glove, rolling towards home plate. Meanwhile, Anderson lost his balance and flew through the air head over heels, landing past the first base bag. Pitcher Carl Pavano raced to retrieve the ball while Anderson tried, unsuccessfully, to get to his feet. Now ensued an amazing sight—a play at first in reverse—with Pavano flipping to Martinez while Anderson dove to the bag from the right-field side. The throw clearly beat him, but the umpire called him safe.

COMMENT

The starting pitcher for the Tigers that day was Armando Galarraga. Less than a year later, another missed call by an umpire in a game involving Galarraga and the Tigers became the stuff of legend. On June 2, 2010, umpire Jim Joyce called the Indians' Jason Donald safe at first, though he seemed clearly out, costing Galarraga a perfect game. Or at least that's what everyone thinks. The truth is murkier. Donald was *not* clearly out at first. He appears clearly out from the replay angle usually shown, with Galarraga's back to the viewer, but from the camera angle showing Galarraga catching the ball, one discerns a slight juggle when the pitcher receives the toss from first baseman Miguel Cabrera. Donald may well have been safe. Certainly, with the bobble taken into account, it was a bang-bang call that could have gone either way. Joyce probably never saw the juggle—he never mentioned it and admitted blowing the call. He may have made the right call for the wrong reason.

Galarraga was unimpressive the rest of the 2010 season and out of the majors for good two years later, finished at the age of 30 with a career record of 26–34 and an ERA of 4.78. Donald, the beneficiary of Joyce's questionable call, was also a heralded prospect who had a surprisingly short and unremarkable career. Like Galarraga, he was out of the big leagues for good after the 2012 season, while just 27.

35: If at First You Don't Succeed...

On April 4, 2001, the Giants and Padres were knotted at 7 in the bottom of the ninth with pinch-runner Calvin Murray on second. Shawon Dunston singled to center, and Murray figured to score to end the game. However, in between second and third, Murray slipped and fell. He got up and sprinted around third, determined to score despite the setback. Mark Kotsay's throw home probably would have beaten Murray easily, but Murray got lucky—he slipped and fell *again*, preventing his ill-advised foray home. But as he beat a hasty retreat to third and dove for the bag, catcher Ben Davis' throw had him beat. However, third baseman Phil Nevin missed the throw, and the ball trickled down the third base line into left field. So Murray picked himself up for the third time and sprinted home, this time without slipping. However, Nevin recovered the ball and threw home to catcher Davis in time to slap on the tag. But just as Nevin failed to handle Davis' throw cleanly, now Davis returned the favor. Murray, the pinch-runner, scored the winning run the hard way.

The Plays

COMMENT

After the game, Murray observed that "I probably haven't slipped twice in 20 years. Tonight I slipped twice in six seconds."[63] All that scrambling and struggling to maintain balance evoked a quarterback evading pass rushers on a mad dash in the backfield. So it is fitting that Murray is the uncle of running quarterback Kyler Murray, of the NFL's Arizona Cardinals.

The next month, Ben Davis, the poor catcher on the play, became involved in a silly controversy. On May 26, 2001, Davis broke up Curt Shilling's perfect game in the eighth inning by laying down a perfect bunt. Diamondbacks players screamed obscenities at him and, after the game, Diamondbacks manager Bob Brenley called the bunt "chickenshit."[64] The incident demonstrated the absurdity of some of baseball's unwritten rules. At the time of Davis' bunt, the Padres trailed the D-backs 2–0. Assuming that the goal in a baseball game is to win, the bunt base hit merited praise. Indeed, Schilling, perhaps rattled by losing his perfect game, walked the next batter and suddenly the Padres, without a base runner for seven innings, were within a base hit of tying the game. Schilling got out of the inning unscathed, gave up two hits in the ninth, and hung on for a 3–1 win. Davis endured unjustified abuse, proving that no good deed goes unpunished.

34: Appeal Denied as Untimely

On April 12, 2009, against the Diamondbacks, in the second inning, trailing by a run, the Dodgers had runners on second and third with one out when Randy Wolf's shot was snared mid-air by pitcher Dan Haren. Haren tossed to second baseman Felipe Lopez, who tagged Juan Pierre for an inning-ending double-play.

After the Diamondbacks left the field, Dodgers manager Joe Torre came out to argue that Andre Ethier, the Dodger runner on third, had touched home plate before the tag on Pierre for the third out. The umpires agreed and awarded the Dodgers a run. But wait. Ethier had not tagged up. He left on contact. The solution was for the Diamondbacks to make an appeal play at third. (Oddly, that would get them a *fourth* out in the inning. A team can indeed record four outs in an inning when they need to in order to prevent an improper run from scoring.) Except it was deemed too late for the Diamondbacks to make an appeal play because they had left the field.

COMMENT

The run counted because of a crazy technicality: The Dodgers convinced the umps to recognize their run after the Diamondbacks had left the field, and the Diamondbacks had no opportunity to challenge that run because ... they had left the field. So, in the Dodgers' 3–1 victory, one of their runs was awarded ex post facto after a line-drive double play. The Associated Press account of the game included this nugget: "Ethier knew he had crossed home plate, but he didn't realize he had scored until he took his position in the outfield for the bottom of the second. 'I still wasn't aware, running out to right field,' Ethier said. 'I see some people talking, and I'm not understanding. And you see a run go up. It was kind of shocking.'"[65]

Torre, famous for many positive things, received nasty treatment in Jim Bouton's *Ball Four*. Bouton relates that ballplayers referred to homely women as "Joe Torre with tits."[66] David Simon, the creator of HBO's brilliant *The Wire*, has cited *Ball Four* as a major influence on him. Serious fans of *Ball Four* and *The Wire* knew that already. *The Wire* incudes several references to the iconic baseball book, including Jimmy McNulty referring to fellow Detective Kima Greggs as "Lester Freamon with tits." In addition, *The Wire* gives catcher Gus Triandos a strange shout-out, as the cop Herc cites Triandos as the one man he would have sex with if forced to make that choice. His reason? Sympathy because Triandos lost five years of his career trying to catch Hoyt Wilhelm's knuckleball.

33: Comedy of Errors

On August 6, 2012, in the top of the eleventh inning, with Roger Bernadina the potential go-ahead run on first, the National's Kurt Suzuki laid down a bunt. Astros first baseman Steve Pearce and pitcher Wilton Lopez, each in hot pursuit, collided, with Pearce winning the fight for the ball. By this time, the pair were joined by third baseman Matt Downs, who did a flying acrobatic move to steer clear of his teammates but may have distracted Pearce, whose errant throw sailed into right field. Bernadina flew around third, ignoring third base coach

Bo Porter's effort to stop him. Astros outfielder Brian Bogusevic threw home to try and nail Bernadina, but airmailed it way over the head of catcher Chris Snyder. Bernadina scored what proved to be the winning run and Suzuki, whose bunt set the chaos in motion, ended up at third.

COMMENT

Suzuki bunted the ball a few feet and ran 270. Absent a crazy foul-up such as this, it is hard for him to get to third base from home plate. He managed just six triples in his 13-year major league career. Pearce, who committed a costly error on this play, is the only player in major league history to hit a pair of walk-off grand slams in less than a week. Bernadina, who scored on the play, did not hit his first career home run until his 51st game. It came in the fourth inning against the Mets on May 12, 2010. He hit his second home run five innings later, a game winner against dominant closer Francisco Rodriguez.

32: *Taylor Made Home Run*

No other inside-the-park home run matches the one credited to the Cubs' Tony Taylor on July 1, 1958. Facing the Giants' Johnny Antonelli in the first inning, Taylor ripped a ground ball inside the third base line that rolled into the Cubs' bullpen in foul territory. The bullpen pitchers and catchers scattered, while left fielder Leon Wagner gave chase. Except a few Cubs in the bullpen spontaneously got down and stared under their bench, leading Wagner to believe the ball was under there. In fact, it had rolled a good fifty feet further down towards the left-field corner where it took refuge by a rain gutter. While Wagner hunted for the ball around the bullpen bench, Taylor cruised the bases for a hidden ball trick inside-the-park home run on a ground ball.

COMMENT

Rain gutter on the field? At least it was in foul territory. A few generations earlier, some ballparks had no outfield fence, and strange items in the outfield (which was often, but not always, separated from the crowd by a rope). Allegedly, in 1892, the speedy Jimmy McAleer, seeking an inside-the-park home run, was tagged out at the plate by a ball wedged in a tomato can. Congress Street Park in Boston was bordered by a garbage dump. You can imagine the rest. But the umpires decided that such a ball cannot be used to record an out. McAleer was credited with a home run. Why doesn't this play make our list of the most bizarre plays? Because it never happened. As Bill Deane observed, the outfielder who allegedly retrieved the ball was Hugh Duffy, but McAleer hit only two home runs against Duffy's teams—neither an inside-the-parker.[67]

Even if his tomato can home run is fictional, McAleer made baseball history with something legitimate—although it, too, reminds us of the unreliability of received history. He is responsible for the tradition of presidents throwing out the first pitch of a season opener. On April 14, 1910, at McAleer's request, President William Howard Taft threw out the first pitch at a game between the Senators and Athletics. After doing his on-field duty, Taft took his seat in the president's box surrounded by other luminaries including Vice President James Sherman. In front of them, Walter Johnson pitched a one-hit shutout. The most memorable play was in the fourth inning, a screaming foul ball off the bat of Home Run Baker (whose double broke up Johnson's no-hitter) that sailed past Taft and careened into the adjacent box, narrowly missing Vice President Sherman before hitting Secretary of the Senate Charles Bennett in the head. Fortunately, Bennett suffered no injuries.

For some reason, word got out that Baker's foul hit Vice President Sherman in the head and knocked him unconscious. You will find that claim in quite a few books, not to mention Sherman's Wikipedia page. Other accounts correctly name Bennett as the recipient of the ball to the head, but virtually all of them call him "Secretary of State"—quite a promotion for the Secretary of the Senate.

 # 31: One-Man Relay

In the third inning of a Blue Jays–White Sox game on August 16, 1987, Toronto's Lloyd Moseby slid into second with a stolen base as Carlton Fisk's throw sailed way over everyone's head into center field. Seeing the flight of the ball, Moseby understandably determined that it had been hit rather than thrown, and feared it might be caught and he'd be doubled off first. He scrambled to his feet and sprinted back to the bag. Kenny Williams' throw from center bounced past first baseman Greg Walker, and Moseby turned tail and shuttled back to second.

Walker, deciding that two bad throws on one play was enough, ate the ball. Meanwhile, Moseby covered 270 feet on the play to progress one base and essentially steal second base twice.

COMMENT

Moseby's day was far from over. He scored that inning on a base hit by George Bell and blasted a two-run home run in the seventh to give Toronto the 6–4 win. Wonder how the official scorer handled Moseby's two-way commute to second? He credited Moseby with a stolen base, even though Moseby gave up the base before reclaiming it. Fisk received no error for the dreadful throw even though it allowed Moseby to return to first (ha-ha). Williams was charged with an error for his throw that skipped past Walker, as it allowed Moseby to return to second. So, if you did not know what happened, and just read the official scoring, you would think that Moseby got to second both by stealing the base *and* by virtue of a throwing error. Which actually makes sense: He did in fact get to second base twice.

30: At Least He Stepped on Third

On June 17, 1962, in the bottom of the first inning against the Cubs, the Mets' Marv Throneberry blasted a triple. When Throneberry was called out on an appeal play for missing first base, Casey Stengel charged out of the dugout to argue—only to be intercepted by Mets first base coach, Cookie Lavagetto, who told Casey not to bother, as Throneberry had missed second too.

COMMENT

The next batter. Charlie Neal, slugged a home run, prompting Stengel to charge from the dugout and emphatically point to all four bases, not taking any chances that Throneberry's disease was contagious.

In a different version of Throneberry's astonishing feat (and feet) of missing two bases, it was the umpires, not Lavagetto, who informed Stengel. What is clear is that Throneberry had one of the worst games in baseball history. Apart from the base-running blunder, he committed three errors, including obstruction that led to a Cubs runner being called safe after the Mets caught him in a rundown. He also went 0–5 (despite the apparent triple) and, for good measure, struck out to end the game with the potential tying run on base.

But you can't keep a good man or team down long, and the Mets and Throneberry had the second game of the doubleheader to redeem themselves. Alas, they lost 4–3. On the first play of the game, Throneberry committed an error on a ground ball.

The losing pitcher in the second game was Wilmer "Vinegar Bend" Mizell, who had one of the great nicknames in baseball history. Mizell, who served three terms in Congress as well as in cabinet posts in the Ford, Reagan, and George H.W. Bush administrations, got the nickname because he was supposedly from the town of Vinegar Bend, Alabama. Except that explains nothing when you think about it (who gets named after his hometown?), especially when you realize that Mizell was actually born in Mississippi. Vinegar Bend was recorded as his birthplace because his family's residence was on that mail route. As of the 2010 census, Vinegar Bend had a population of 192. Mizell remains its most famous near-resident.

Back to Throneberry. Plays like his infamous "missed two bases on a triple" gave him the reputation as a lovable loser, but the loser part is somewhat unfair. On his career, Throneberry hit a respectable 53 home runs in 1,186 at-bats and never committed more than five errors in a season. And in Triple A, he was a veritable terror, twice hitting 40 or more home runs in a season.

29: Kick Save and a Beauty

Outfielders (and for that matter infielders) kicking the ball? Happens all the time. Outfielders *deliberately* kicking the ball? Pretty rare. Outfielders deliberately kicking the ball and hitting the cutoff man to prevent a run from scoring? That could *never* happen. Except it did. With the Phils and Reds in the tenth inning on July 5, 1989, and Steve Jeltz on second base with the potential winning run, Lenny Dykstra singled to right. A charging Paul O'Neill bobbled the ball, which fell to the ground, and O'Neill figured the game was over. In frustration he wound up and kicked the ball full force. The ball went right to the cutoff man, first baseman Todd Benzinger, and Jeltz had to hold at third.

COMMENT

As it happens, two batters later Jeltz scored on a passed ball for the walk-off win. Jeltz, a switch-hitter, once hit home runs from both sides of the plate in a game he did not start. Which is especially remarkable considering that he hit a total of five home runs in his eight-year career. That game, a 15–11 Phillies win over the Pirates in Philadelphia on June 8, 1989, is better known for something unrelated. After the Pirates plated 10 runs in the first inning, their broadcaster, Jim Rooker, said on the air, "If we lose this game, I'll walk home." The Pirates somehow did lose, and Rooker kept his word. After the season, he conducted a 300-mile charity walk from Philadelphia to Pittsburgh.

Rooker also did something notable as a player. He was a pretty good hitting pitcher, managing a lifetime batting average of .201. He also slugged seven home runs. Impressive but hardly sensational. (Wes Farrell hit 37; Warren Spahn and Bob Lemon 35 each.) What is remarkable is that four of Rooker's home runs came in a single season, in just 57 at bats. Two came in consecutive at-bats against Jim Kaat. (Kaat got even by mashing a three-run double, and Rooker actually lost the game in which he homered twice.) That was Rooker's rookie year. He followed that up by hitting just three home runs in the next 12 years and 600 at-bats.

Rooker losing a game in which he slugged two home runs is a candidate for Most Bittersweet Performance, but gives way to Brad Penny's outing on May 21, 2010. Pitching for the Cardinals, Penny got roughed up by the Angels, allowing four runs in the second inning. He redeemed himself in the third, slugging a grand slam that lifted the Cardinals to a 9–4 lead. Penny wouldn't get the win, however, nor any wins for the rest of the season: On his grand slam, he tore a lat muscle and spent the rest of the season on the disabled list.

A similar but even worse fate befell Jim Edmonds on September 21, 2010. He belted a home run but tore his Achilles in the process—a career-ending blow.

28: Umpire Deception

On July 20, 1947, the Cardinals led the Dodgers 2–0 after eight innings. It looked like they had padded their lead in the top of the ninth when Ron Northey's blast to center eluded a leaping Pete Reiser and briefly disappeared before returning to the playing field. The first base umpire, Larry Goetz, believing the ball struck the top of the wall, signaled that it was in play. As Northey raced to third, he saw the third base umpire, Beans Reardon, signal that the ball was in fact a home run, believing (incorrectly) that it reached the crowd before dropping back on to the field. Northey slowed to a trot, but the Dodgers did not. Right fielder Dixie Walker retrieved the ball and fired to cut-off man Eddie Stanky, who relayed it home to catcher Bruce Edwards. Northey, spurred by this activity around him, resumed a sprint and slid into home, but was called out by Jocko Conlon. It may seem that this play, however bizarre, doesn't merit the high rating I've given it. But the aftermath makes the play special. Keep reading.

COMMENT

Northey's blunder wouldn't have much mattered except the Dodgers' bats finally came alive in the bottom half, and they scored three runs for the walk-off victory. The Cardinals protested, and their protest was *upheld* by National League president Ford Frick. The umpires informed Frick that Northey would have scored had he not slowed up, and Frick essentially invoked the unwritten rule of "umpire deception." Had Frick played it by the book, the game would have resumed from the point of the screw-up, with the Cardinals thus reclaiming the lead, 3–0, and the Dodgers' three-run ninth wiped off the books. Frick instead chose a common-sense compromise, keeping the Dodgers' three runs in the ninth and declaring the game a 3–3 tie. (It is unclear why the teams did not resume play at a future date.)

Recall that a similar "umpire deception" compromise led to a triple-play reduced to a double-play in Game 4 of the 1980 NLDS. See Play # 40. As it happens, in both situations the problem stemmed in part from two or more umpires making conflicting rulings during the play. Ditto Play # 53.

By odd coincidence, Goetz and Reardon, whose conflicting calls sparked the chaos, were two of the three umpires featured in the famous Norman Rockwell painting, *Bottom of the Sixth*.

27: *Tasty Pickle*

On June 19, 1991, in the sixth inning against the Phillies, the Braves had Greg Olson on third and Rafael Belliard on first. On a suicide squeeze with both runners going, Tom Glavine fanned on the bunt. Olson headed back to third, where the throw from catcher Steve Lake had him beat, but third baseman Charlie Hayes missed the tag. At about this time Belliard arrived at third. Seeing that his teammate already occupied the bag, he turned and started running back to second. With Belliard in a rundown between second and third, Olson again broke home, but the Phils threw home and, for the second time on the play, Olson was caught in a rundown between third and home. Once again, he made it safely to third where, once again, he met Belliard. This time, Belliard was tagged out and Olson allowed to remain at third.

COMMENT

Belliard was credited with a stolen base and a caught stealing on the same play!

Glavine was no doubt kicking himself for costing his team a run and an out by not getting the bunt down. (He was a terrific bunter who laid down 15 sacrifices that year and once led the American League with 17.) No problem. He proceeded to drive in Olson with a base hit—his third of the game. Glavine also pitched eight innings, allowed no earned runs and struck out twelve. An extraordinary all-around performance less memorable than the unique event set in motion by his failed bunt attempt.

26: *Long and Winding Road*

On May 27, 2003, with the game tied 2–2 in the bottom of the Ninth, the Giants' Rubén Rivera was on first when Marquis Grissom blasted a ball to deep right-centerfield that Diamondbacks outfielder David Dellucci leaped for but missed. Rivera, who had made it to second by the time the ball came down, mistakenly thought Dellucci had caught the ball. He started to sprint back to first, but quickly realized his mistake, turned around and headed in the right direction. But to compensate for time lost, Rivera cut across the diamond toward third, bypassing second by several feet. He quickly realized this mistake too, and returned to second, before resuming his trip to third. He had lost so much time that he was out by a mile at third, except the low throw was kicked by third baseman Alex Cintron and rolled back toward second base. Rivera decided not to leave well enough alone, and headed home hoping for the game-ending run, but he was again out by a mile and finally put out of his misery by catcher Rod Barajas' tag.

COMMENT

The play is made even more bizarre by the fact that Rivera has just been inserted into the game as a pinch-runner. And Giants broadcaster Jon Miller helped make the play unforgettable. In real time, Miller excitedly proclaimed this "the worst base-running in the history of the game." Rivera played the next day, and then retired, perhaps satisfied that he had immortalized himself (in case being Mariano Rivera's cousin wasn't enough).

That said, Miller's claim that this was the worst base-running in the history of the game was overstated. That honor belongs to Jimmy St. Vrain, at least if we're to believe a story told by Davy Jones in *The Glory of Their Times*.[68] St. Vrain, a pitcher who threw left and batted right, was so poor at the plate that his manager suggested he try batting left-handed. He did so, and after slapping a weak groundball to short, out of confusion he ran to third base. The shortstop, Honus Wagner, not thrown off by St Vrain's adventure, threw to first. If this actually happened (I've been unable to verify it), St. Vrain was thrown out at first by almost 180 feet.

Here is how the *Los Angeles Times* described vaguely similar base-running in a 1911 game between the Senators and Highlanders:

[Germany] Schaefer rolled a slow one down the first base line toward Hal Chase. The latter was about to tag Schaefer out, but 'Germany' had an inspiration. He put on the reverse and turned backward toward home, with Chase after him. 'Germany' touched home, but didn't stop. He set sail for third, Chase still in pursuit. After rounding third and aiming toward second, the situation proved too much for him. Holding his aching sides, he fell to the ground, Chase tripping over him. The two lay there a full minute.[69]

Yet another similar play allegedly occurred in 1893. Brooklyn's Con Daily was supposedly chased back to third during a rundown, but the base was already occupied by his teammate, Oyster Burns. Daily took an unusual approach to this unfortunate circumstance, rounding third in reverse and heading for second—overrunning a teammate in the wrong direction. The puzzled catcher continued his pursuit of Daily, then threw to second but too late to get Daily. Until the umpires straightened things out (calling Daily out), Daily and Burns stood on second and third respectively—having switched bases from the previous play.

Daily and Burns were both born in 1864 (five days apart) and died in 1928 in Brooklyn. Uncanny? Of course not. Such coincidences excite people who aren't thinking clearly. (John Wilkes Booth and Lee Harvey Oswald both have 15 letters in their name!) Just consider that Burns and Dailey died at the age of 64, a normal lifespan for the time. *Tons* of people born in 1864 died in 1928.

The Daily/Burns non-coincidence calls to mind a sports phenomenon that really is uncanny—when two teammates are so similar in talent, physique, role, history, and even uniform number that they become indistinguishable. Let's call this concept "Luce-Ramsey" after its best exemplars, hockey players Craig Ramsey and Don Luce. Or was it *Don* Ramsey and *Craig* Luce? The two played on the same Buffalo Sabres' checking line and killed penalties together throughout the 1970s. Since they were a superb penalty-killing duo, and defended brilliantly against the other team's best scoring line, every discussion about the Sabres noted "Luce and Ramsey." Never just Luce or Ramsey—always "Luce *and* Ramsey" as a single unit with no differentiation between the members. One wore #10, the other #20, and apart from serious Sabres fans, no one knew which was which.

Runner-up for best Luce-Ramsey was a pair of NBA players: Cliff Levingston and Antoine Carr. Eventually they were traded to different teams and established their own identities, but for a period of years Levingston and Carr were eerily intertwined. Both were substitute forwards for the Atlanta Hawks who could score, rebound, and defend but couldn't pass or dribble. Carr was listed as 6'9", Levingston a non-discernible inch shorter. They were each first round picks by the Pistons (Levingston the 8th overall in 1982, Carr the 9th the following year) but traded—together—in 1985 to the Hawks, where each spent five years. One wore #35, the other #53. Levingston and Carr seemed interchangeable even apart from both having attended college at relatively obscure Wichita State. But no, they were not identical twins separated at birth—they were born six months apart. In case you're wondering, former NBA player Cory Carr is not related to Antoine. He is, however, Levingston's cousin.

What is baseball's best Luce–Ramsey? Easy answer: Rich Coggins and Al Bumbry. In 1972, the pair excelled as partners in the outfield of the Rochester Red Wings, the Orioles' Triple A affiliate. In September, the Birds brought up the promising pair for a cup of coffee: Bumbry played in nine games and batted .364; Coggins played in 16 and batted .333. In 1973, both blossomed: The speedy lefty Coggins batted .319 and stole 17 bases whereas the speedy lefty Bumbry batted .337 and stole 23 bases. Playing only against right-handed pitchers in Earl Weaver's platoon, each played in 110 games and slugged seven home runs. Bumbry wore #1, Coggins #2. Throughout the season, accounts of O's games featured passages like this from the *New York Times*: "Bumbry and Coggins or Coggins and Bumbry, the Orioles' rookie outfielding firm.... The two little men, who are not used against left-handed pitchers, were responsible for the Orioles tying the game in the first."[70] It gets eerier. On May 9, playing in his 23rd career game, Bumbry led off the ninth with his first career home run. Up strode Coggins, playing in his 25th career game and, you guessed it, slugged his first career home run. It was only the second time in baseball history that two players each hit their first career home runs back to back.

Surely Bumbry's and Coggins' careers diverged the next year? Nope, they were both sophomore busts: Bumbry hit just .233, with a poor on-base percentage of .304; Coggins slipped to .243, with an on-base percentage of .299. Thereafter, it was all downhill for Coggins, whereas Bumbry had some decent seasons. But for more than two years, the two had nearly identical careers ... in identical bodies: Both stood 5'8" and tipped the scales at 170 pounds.

Seventh Inning Stretch

It is no accident that the commentary following Play # 26 was so long. I wanted to give readers a break before delivering you the most bizarre 25 plays in baseball history. These must be savored. We have to this point seen some of everything—fluky triple plays and inside-the-park home runs, little league–like rundowns, insane rules and calls and arguments, the surreal involvement of fans and bat boys and much more. What could possibly outdo these plays to make the top 25?

25: *Marty and Steve's Wonderful Adventure*

Imagine a play resembling the Ruben Rivera fiasco that Jon Miller called the worse base-running play in the history of the game, except involving *two* players and ending spectacularly well for their team. On May 18, 1986, the Red Sox trailed the Rangers, 4–3 in the bottom of the 10th with one out, Steve Lyons on second and Marty Barrett at the plate. Barrett smacked a base hit down the line in right that a diving George Wright could not quite corral. Lyons mistakenly thinking that Wright caught the ball, raced back to second base. Just as he slid into the bag, Barrett arrived standing up. To alleviate the logjam, Lyons again headed for third. Wright's wild throw to third bounced into the dugout, allowing both runners to score and giving the Red Sox an undeserved and wacky walk-off win.

COMMENT

The next day's Associated Press included this priceless quote from Wright: "I saw two guys at second and threw the ball to third. Now that I think of it, maybe I should've thrown to second."[71]

Any play involving Steve Lyons evokes memories of an infamous incident involving him on July 16, 1990. After sliding headfirst into first base to beat out a bunt, Lyons felt pebbles in his pants. He did the obvious thing: He pulled his pants down to empty them—oblivious to the thousands of people (and countless more on television) watching his striptease. The sliding shorts Lyons wore under his uniform diminished the embarrassment *a little*. At the end of the inning, as he came in to the dugout, women in the stands waved dollar bills at him and screamed at Lyons to take it off.

Almost any book about baseball history should include a mention or two of the 1986 World Series. Now is a good time, since Play # 25, featuring good Red Sox luck, occurred just five months before the tragic Red Sox collapse. What more is there to say about the tenth inning meltdown culminating in Bill Buckner's mishap? Only this: Almost everyone remembers it incorrectly.

Stephen Jay Gould shrewdly observed that most people remember

Buckner's error as coming with the Red Sox ahead in Game 7.[72] That's doubly mistaken; the game was tied and it was Game 6. The significance? On the widely believed but incorrect version, the Red Sox would have won the World Series had Buckner fielded Mookie Wilson's routine ground ball. In reality, Game 6 would have remained tied. On the incorrect version, Buckner's misplay meant the Mets won the series. In reality, the Red Sox still had Game 7 to redeem themselves. Gould argues, convincingly, that the widespread mis-recollection of the play reflects the human tendency to tidy up narratives, to make them simpler and more satisfying.

24: Umpire Omission = Triple-Play

On May 2, 2017, in the eighth inning against the Orioles, the Red Sox, seeking to extend their 5–2 lead, had Mitch Moreland on second, Dustin Pedroia on first, nobody out, and Jackie Bradley, Jr., at bat. Bradley Jr. lofted a routine pop that took Orioles shortstop J.J. Hardy into shallow left. Thinking it was an easy catch, Moreland and Pedroia stayed close to their respective bags. Thinking the infield fly rule would be in effect (making him an automatic out), Bradley Jr. did not leave the batter's box. But Hardy somehow fanned on the catch. He quickly picked up the ball and threw to second baseman Jonathan Schoop who tagged out Moreland, who had wandered off the bag. Schoop then stepped on second to force out Pedroia (who never left first), and threw to first to get Bradley. Triple-play.

COMMENT

The key to this play is the umpires did *not* invoke the infield fly rule. That meant that, when the ball dropped, the force play was available at third and second—bad news for the Red Sox. But it also meant Bradley was not automatically out—bad news for Baltimore, except Bradley Jr. did not run. And if you still don't understand what happened, take it from me: Announcers Bob Costas and John Smoltz, a terrific play-by-play guy and Hall of Fame pitcher respectively, did no better trying to explain it. This much we know: The missing of a routine pop-up resulted in a triple-play.

The play illustrates a quirk of the infield fly rule. The rule was designed to assist the team at bat but can assist the team in the field instead. Worse still, it does so by rewarding poor play. The rule purportedly guards against infielders deliberately dropping pop-ups in order to get a double-play. But while it is unclear how many cheap double-plays the rule prevents, it rewards the defense whenever a pop fly is missed, giving them the automatic out despite the blunder.

Whether or not the rule is invoked, you do not often (as in ever, apart from this play) get a triple-play on an infield fly. This plays calls to mind the aphorism "I'd rather be lucky than good," which, as noted, is usually credited to the offbeat pitcher Lefty Gomez. Gomez was a first-rate quipster, akin to Yogi Berra *deliberately* being funny. After undergoing triple bypass surgery, Gomez remarked that it was "the first triple of my career."[73] He wasn't kidding. In 1,023 plate appearances spanning 14 seasons, Gomez never hit a triple—or, for that matter, a home run.

Joe Niekro, the knuckleballer, was almost as futile as Gomez at the plate. He managed exactly one triple and one home run in his 1,165 career at bats. The home run came against … his brother Phil. Phil was also a knuckleballer and, yes, the momentous sibling home run was off a knuckleball. Some might suspect the fix was in, that big brother grooved the pitch so little Joe might experience the joy of a home run. If that was your reaction, you don't have a brother.

The game was on May 29, 1976, and the box score belies any suspicion of collusion. Joe's homer came in the seventh inning and tied the score at 2. The Astros added a pair in the eighth, and won 4–3. Joe got the win (along with eternal bragging rights), Phil took the loss. Zero-sum game for the Niekro parents.

23: Diversionary Tactics

In a game against the Dodgers on June 17, 1926, the Cubs had the bases loaded with one out in the sixth inning. With Jimmy Cooney on first, Joe Kelly grounded to first baseman Babe Herman. Herman threw to shortstop Rabbit Maranville covering second to retire Cooney but Maranville's return throw to first was wild. When Brooklyn pitcher Jesse Barnes, backing up first, retrieved the ball, he saw a Cub sprinting home so he fired the ball to catcher Mickey O'Neil. But as O'Neil went to make the tag, the runner detoured to the Cubs' dugout. O'Neil pursued him until he realized that the runner was Cooney, who had been forced out at second earlier in the play (but just kept running). With the Cubs diverted by Cooney, the batter Kelly made it to third.

COMMENT

Note that a player who attempted what Cooney did today would probably be declared out: Rule 7.09 says it is batter or runner interference when: "(e) any batter or runner who has just been retired hinders or impedes any following play being made on a runner. Such runner shall be declared out for the interference of a teammate." In fact, we will shortly see an example of this rule in action.

O'Neill, an obscure player (he hit .238 with four homers in eleven seasons), was involved in two of the most bizarre plays in baseball history. The other, which is still forthcoming, was just two months after the above play. On the above play, he was not given an error for allowing Kelly to reach third. It probably was not a case of a generous official scorer—the game featured twelve errors by the two teams. Which, to be sure, was less unusual in those days. Maranville, who was charged an error on the play, committed 46 on the year—an improvement over the previous three years (when he committed 65, 55, and 50). And he was considered a great defensive shortstop. In fairness, gloves in those days were nothing like modern gloves.

Cooney, incidentally, pulled off one of the 14 unassisted triple-plays in baseball history. That comes out to roughly one every 12 seasons. And yet, the day after Cooney managed the feat on May 30, 1927, a player named Johnny Neun did the same. Neun's came in the ninth inning to end a 1–0 game in favor of his Tigers. Five weeks after his defensive coup, Neun had a five-hit, five stolen base game. So why have you never heard of this guy? Well, consistency was not his thing. Here are his batting averages for 1927–30: .324, .213, .325, .221.

Billy Wambsganss pulled off by far the most famous unassisted triple-play, because it came in a World Series—Game 5 of the 1920 fall classic. Wambsganss' solo tri-killing slammed shut a Brooklyn Robins' rally, and maybe demoralized the Robins. After that play, the Robins scored 1 run in 22 innings, and fell to the Indians in seven games. The unassisted triple-play overshadowed one of the great World Series performances: Cleveland's Jim Bagby pitched the complete game victory, allowing just one run, and blasted a three-run homer to help his cause. It was a dream season all around for Bagby, who led the league with 31 wins and 48 complete games. But he may have thrown out his arm in the process. The next year Bagby won just 14 games and saw his ERA rise from 2.89 (the previous year) to .470. He won seven games total over the next two years, while his ERA ballooned further, and was out of the majors for good at the age of 33.

22: Duped and Deked by Dukes

On June 6, 2009, in the fourth inning the Mets trailed the Nationals 3–0. With Luis Castillo on first for the Mets, Emil Brown drove the ball to right where Elijah Dukes seemed to make a sliding catch. The umpire ruled the ball a trap, but Castillo didn't see that and returned to first, crossing paths with Brown who headed for second and implored Castillo to do the same. Castillo, who by this point was almost all the way back to first, reversed course and headed back toward second. Meanwhile, from flat on his back, Dukes threw the ball in to the infield, where first baseman Nick Johnson scooped it up and threw to second in time to get Castillo. Brown was called out for passing Castillo, and a seeming fly-out became a seeming base hit that became a strong candidate for the strangest double-play in major league history. (But see Play # 14.)

COMMENT

Castillo had one of baseball's longest hitting streaks, 35, snapped with him in the on-deck circle. You'd think he would have been okay with that, insofar as the game ended on a walk-off win for his Marlins. But while his teammates celebrated raucously, Castillo remained in the on-deck circle, looking distraught. Manager Jeff Torborg came over to console him.

In fairness, Joe DiMaggio's 56-game hitting streak is so ballyhooed that having a long hitting streak snapped can bring out the worst in a player. When the Braves' Gene Garber struck out Pete Rose with a breaking ball in the ninth inning to end Rose's 44 game hitting streak, Rose complained that Garber didn't challenge him with fastballs. Which, if you think about it, is ridiculous.

Back to Castillo. The Mets allegedly suggested that the switch-hitter stick to batting right-handed, with good reason: He was exponentially more powerful from the right side—on his career, an extra base hit for every 12.5 at-bats batting righty versus one every 33 at bats as a lefty. (If we stick to home runs, the disparity is greater still: one for every 69 at bats versus one for every 1,600 at bats.) Castillo is hardly alone. Quite a few switch-hitters bat from both sides only because they can, not because it makes sense. Jarrod Saltalamacchia (whose 14-letter last name is the longest in baseball history) was always much better from the left side, with the discrepancy ridiculous in 2013. Fenway Park is supposed to help righties, but don't tell Salty: From the left side, the Red Sox backstop hit .294, with a slugging percentage of .513 and 12 home runs in 306 at bats—all-star numbers for a catcher. From the right side, he batted .218 with just two home runs in 106 at-bats. At a certain point, it might have been worth trying batting right-handed all the time.

21: In the Nick of Time

In the seventh inning of the Padres–Diamondbacks game on September 15, 2009, the Diamondbacks trailed 2–1 and had Brandon Allen on first. On Eric Byrne's long double, the Padres' shortstop, Everth Cabrera, threw home trying to nail Allen. The throw bounced off catcher Nick Hundley and rolled towards the Diamondbacks' dugout. If the ball made it to the dugout, Byrnes, now racing towards third, would be awarded home. Desperate to avoid that result, Hundley sprinted after the ball and arrived just in time to corral it while he slid. However, his momentum was taking him into the dugout. Before sliding down the dugout steps, he flipped the ball from his glove on to the field. Then he climbed the steps, retrieved the ball, and threw home trying to get the charging Byrnes. First baseman Adrian Gonzalez raced in to cover the plate, arriving at the same time as Byrnes, but Hundley's rushed throw short-hopped him. Gonzalez made a sliding pick-up and slap tag in one motion to nail Byrnes, a fittingly dazzling end to a play featuring the catcher sliding into the dugout and the first baseman sliding into home.

COMMENT

The brilliant defensive play kept the score tied at 2, but went for naught when a Mark Reynolds home run in the ninth won the game for

Arizona. That year, Reynolds had an all-or-nothing year for the ages, slugging 44 home runs while striking out 223 times in 578 at-bats. When you factor in his 76 walks, fewer than 50 percent of his plate appearances resulted in a batted ball that didn't leave the ballpark.

Notwithstanding the impressive agility he showed on this play, Hundley is a typical catcher, meaning not fleet of foot. (He did steal a base in this very game, but just 15 in his career.) He managed only 20 triples in a 974-game career—one triple every 487 games. That is normal for a catcher. The odds-defying part is that four of those triples came in a six-game span (in 2015). I have no explanation other than weird stuff happens.

Another catcher, Clyde McCullough, slugged three home runs in one game (on July 26, 1942), though the rest of the season he hit two in 334 at bats and he never hit more than nine in his 15-year career. Sadly, on the day of his miraculous outburst, McCullough accounted for all the Cubs runs in a 4–3 defeat, hitting solo home runs in his first three at-bats. In the ninth inning, with the score tied at three and a runner on first, McCullough had a chance to win the game and join the truly exclusive club of players who hit four consecutive home runs. He popped out to first. In the bottom of the inning, the Phils' Danny Litwhiler doubled and came around to score the walk-off run. That season, Litwhiler became the first major leaguer ever to play every game in a season and not commit an error. (His glove is on display in Cooperstown.) The previous season, he committed 15. Like I said, weird stuff happens.

20: *The Great Borkowski At-Bat*

On September 22, 1954, in the ninth inning the Braves' ace Warren Spahn was protecting a 3–1 lead against the Reds. With runners on first and second and one out, Spahn fanned Bob Borkowski, but the ball got past catcher Del Crandall. Crandall retrieved it and threw to third-baseman Eddie Mathews too late to nail the runner, Gus Bell. Mathews immediately fired to first, hoping to beat the batter, Borkowski. This was a bad idea, since Borkowski was already out—with first base occupied and less than two outs, a strikeout is an automatic out even if the third strike is not caught by the catcher. Worse still, Mathews' gratuitous throw hit Borkowski and sailed into right field. Bell and Wally Post (who started the play at first base) scampered around for two runs to tie the score 3–3. However, the umpires declared that Borkowski's pointless venture toward first base, which drew Mathews' throw, constituted illegal interference. Thus, the play resulted in a double-play with both outs by Borkowski, one for striking out and one for interference—call it "illegal inducement of a throw." The crazy play ended the game, preserving the Braves' 3–1 victory. Or so it seemed.

COMMENT

The umpires' decision was reasonable, but the National League president, Warren Giles, granted the Reds' protest and ordered the game replayed from the point of the mishap. Giles claimed that Borkowski's improper action in running to first was not sufficient to justify calling an out. It was sufficiently improper, however, to freeze the play before Mathews made the throw. In other words, Giles split the difference between the two runs scoring and two outs being recorded. He said Post and Bell should have been returned to third base and second respectively and the score should have remained 3–1. Giles ordered the game resumed on September 24, two days later.

When the game resumed, Braves manager Charlie Grimm replaced Spahn on the mound with Dave Jolly and Reds manager Birdie Tebbets sent Nino Escalera in to pinch-run for Post at second base. On the first pitch of the resumed game, Johnny Temple singled to center. When center fielder Billy Bruton bobbled the ball, the speedy Escalera scampered home to tie the game 3–3. However, the Braves scored in the bottom of the inning to win the strange game a second time.

A seemingly odd feature of the game was that Spahn, the Braves ace, had entered the game in the ninth in relief. Spahn actually pitched in relief five times that season. In fact, during his 21-year career, there were any number of years where he pitched a handful of games in relief. In addition to his 363 career wins, he notched 28 saves. Giles' decision to replay the game cost him a 29th. It also cost Ernie Johnson (who pitched eight sterling innings) the win, which instead went to Jolly (who faced two batters and allowed a game-tying single). Two years later, Johnson's wife gave birth to Ernie Johnson, Jr., the likable TNT sportscaster. From 1993 through 1996, father and son Johnsons broadcast Braves games together.

If Spahn was an ace starter who occasionally relieved, Jolly was a reliever who occasionally started. And by occasionally, I mean *once* in his career. (He relieved in 158 games.) That one start, also in 1954, was brilliant: He held the Brooklyn Dodgers (whose lineup included Jackie Robinson, Roy Campanella, Duke Snider, Gil Hodges, and Carl Furillo) to one run and four hits over ten innings. It is odd, to say the least, that the 29-year-old never again started a game.

Whereas Spahn never stopped starting (so to speak): In five seasons *after he turned 40*, he started 30 or more games. He won 20 in two of those seasons. For good measure, he pitched two no-hitters after turning 39.

19: Can't Anyone Here Run the Bases?

On April 22, 2016, with the bases loaded and no outs in the seventh inning, a line drive by the Rangers' Mitch Moreland was caught by White Sox right fielder Adam Eaton. Meanwhile, *all three* Rangers runners screwed up. Ian Desmond on first broke to second, and Eaton's throw behind him should have doubled him off. However, the bad throw pulled Jose Abreu off the base. Desmond made it back safely but overran the bag. Abreu turned to tag Desmond, but Desmond did an elusive dance. Abreu managed to dive and tag Desmond out and, from his knees fired home in case Prince Fielder, the runner on third, had any ideas. But Fielder, who should have tagged up and scored on the original play, retreated to third where he met his teammate, Adrian Beltre—who, seeing that Fielder did not tag up, should have remained at second. A few throws and rundowns later, Todd Frazier tagged out Fielder to complete the 9–3–2–6–2–5 triple-play.

COMMENT

Beltre was involved in the next play on our list as well. It is not entirely surprising that he was involved in two of the most bizarre plays of all-time, not to mention shows up in the comment section after another play for a crazy ejection. Beltre is nothing if not colorful. He hit many home runs while somehow dropping to a knee, which seems impossible. He insisted on playing third base without a cup and, as a result, once spent time on the disabled list with testicular bleeding. (When he returned from the DL, the PA system at Safeco Field greeted his stroll to the plate with music from the Nutcracker Suite.) Beltre *hated* when teammates massaged his head, which assured that they did so at every opportunity.

Fielder, the last man standing for the Rangers on the play, hit 319 career home runs. His father, Cecil, hit 319 as well. Prince hit 50 once in his 12-year career; Cecil hit 50 (actually 51) once in his 13-year career. But Prince wasn't just a chip off the old block. Though 45 pounds heavier than Dad (275 to 230), he was the superior base-stealer: He managed 18 thefts whereas Cecil managed a mere two, both in 1996. After the first, Cecil declared that "I've been working on my jumps for nine years."[74]

Desmond, the other hapless base runner on the play, started his career in style after paying his dues in the minors for six years. In his big-league debut, September 10, 2009, he belted a double and home run and drove in four runs in the Nats' 8–7 win. The Phils almost spoiled things in the ninth, scoring five runs and putting two men on base with one out, but shortstop Desmond turned the pivot on a game-ending double-play. In his next start, two days later, he went 4–4 with a walk. In his next two starts, four more hits. Not surprisingly, the September call-up never saw another minor league stadium.

18: Amazing Chase

On July 12, 2007, in the fifth inning with the bases loaded against the Tigers, the Mariners' Beltre singled into right field, scoring two runs. When the Tigers threw home trying to catch the trail runner, Beltre headed for second base. Catcher Mike Rabelo threw to shortstop Carlos Guillen ahead of Beltre. Beltre slid around Guillen's tag but the slide carried him well past second base. Guillen lunged to tag him, but Beltre again eluded him and found the bag. Umpire Bruce Froemming signaled him safe. Not satisfied with this success, Beltre inexplicably sprung to his feet and raced for third. Guillen chased after him but dropped the ball en route. Amidst all this attention paid to Beltre, Richie Sexson, who started the play at first, scampered home to give Seattle their third run on the play. However, the Tigers appealed that Beltre missed second base and Froemming (who had signaled Beltre safe) decided they were right and called him out. The three runs still counted.

COMMENT

The runs scored by the Mariners during the chaos were their only runs of the game. And just enough, as they won 3–2. J.J. Putz, the Mariners' closer who slammed the door in the ninth, pitched in 572 games in the big leagues without a single start. Which left him only 547 games short of the record—1,119 by John Franco. Franco was primarily a starter in the minors, and Putz even more so. In his first four seasons, he started 87 games and pitched in relief only twice.

One of the Mariners to score on the play, aided by Carlos Guillen's error, was Jose Guillen—no relation. The name meld pales in comparison to the home run the Dodgers' Will Smith hit in Game 5 of the 2020 NLCS off the Braves' Will Smith.

17: Uncanny Manny

On July 21, 2004, against the Red Sox, the Orioles had a runner on third with two outs in the seventh inning and David Newhan facing Pedro Martinez. Newhan drove a fly ball off the wall. Centerfielder Johnny Damon chased after the ball as it rolled toward left field. Damon finally retrieved the ball, and tried to hit the cutoff man, shortstop Mark Bellhorn. Something unforeseeable got in the way—Red Sox left fielder Manny Ramirez. Ramirez inexplicably cut off Damon's throw with a diving catch! Manny scrambled to his feet and tossed the ball to Bellhorn, who threw home, but too late. Newhan took advantage of Manny's unique cut-off, scampering home for an inside-the-park home run.

COMMENT

There is a reason outfielders aren't supposed to throw to outfielders—three throws on a play is one too many. What was Ramirez thinking? Nothing at all. Just Manny being Manny as they used to say in Boston. This was Manny at his Mannyest.

Another Manny being Manny moment, with the man again doing something players simply aren't supposed to do, came in a 2008 game against the Orioles in Camden Yards. Ramirez made a spectacular catch in deep left to rob his old teammate, Kevin Millar. Though there was a runner on base, Manny did not try to stop his momentum and throw the ball back in, like any normal outfielder would. He kept going the wrong way, running up to the wall and high-fiving a fan in the crowd before turning and firing the ball to Dustin Pedroia. Notwithstanding Manny's leisure activities, Pedroia's relay to Kevin Youkilis doubled off Aubrey Huff. In a single play, Ramirez made a great catch, notched an outfield assist, and accepted congratulations from a fan in between the two.

Newhan, the beneficiary of Ramirez' crazy diving cut-off, lasted eight seasons in the big leagues, primarily as a second baseman. His path to that position was unusual. Newhan played outfield until his Class A manager Jim Colborn needed a second baseman after the team's regular second baseman was injured. The night of the injury, Colborn noticed in the team's parking lot a car with the license plate, "LV2TRN2" (presumably short for "loves to train"). He asked the team which player owned that car. Newhan acknowledged ownership.

"Get your infield glove, you're going to be a second baseman," Colborn said.[75]

16: Déjà vu All Over Again and Again and Again

When last we encountered David Hulse, he was laughing in the outfield with Jose Canseco after the latter headed a ball over the fence for a home run. Just seven months earlier, Hulse himself provided the laughs. On October 3, 1992, the season finale for the Angels and Rangers, in the ninth inning the left-handed Hulse scattered the Angels by slapping a foul ball into their dugout on the third-base side. On the next pitch, he fouled a ball in the identical spot, again causing the Angels to scramble; a police officer, who for some reason was in the dugout, waved a white towel in surrender. But Hulse wasn't done. On the next pitch, he fouled off *another* pitch in the same spot! Two is a coincidence, three is a trend. By now, the Angel players and coaches crouched together at the other end of the dugout. On the next pitch, Hulse did it *again*, a fourth straight foul ball to the same spot in the dugout, which by this point was vacated. Now the Angel players gave him an ovation.

COMMENT

Hulse wasn't done making baseball history. Two years later he hit the only inside-the-park home run Mariano Rivera allowed in his 19-year career.

Hulse's four-foul-balls into the dugout, like Tim McCarver's two foul balls that hit Alice Roth, were not technically a single play, but they were so good that I made exceptions and included them in the 150 Most Bizarre Plays. A few other plays (including the #1, still to come!) were also too good to keep out even though they were plays (plural) rather than a single play. I admit to inconsistency in not including Tippy Martinez picking off three Blue Jays in the tenth inning on August 24, 1983. But that story needs telling.

During that game, a combination of injuries and over-managing left the Orioles without a catcher. As the Birds headed out for the tenth inning, Lenn Sakata donned the gear despite having never caught a game in his life. (In an eleven-year career, he played in 564 games, mostly at second and short.) After a Cliff Johnson home run and Barry Bonnell single chased Tim Stoddard, Tippy Martinez was brought in to pitch. With Bonnell looking forward to stealing on the non-catcher catcher, Martinez picked him off first. The next two batters also reached first, also expected to steal, and also got picked off by Martinez!

Can't get any crazier, right? Of course it can. In the bottom of the tenth, the Orioles tied the game on a leadoff home run by Cal Ripken, then won it on a three-run walk-off home run by ... catcher extraordinaire, Lenn Sakata.

15: Leaving Home for Good

In a Spring Training game on March 29, 1954, the Cardinals, with runners on first and third, sent the runner on first, Tom Alston, for a steal of second. The plan was for the runner on third, Joe Frazier, to break home when the White Sox threw down to second. But the Sox outsmarted the Cards with the old little league play: Catcher Red Wilson's throw was intercepted (by design) by pitcher Bob Keegan. Keegan returned the ball to Wilson while Frazier was halfway between third and home. Wilson chased Frazier down and tagged him near third. By this time, Alston was whirling toward third, and just kept on chugging. Wilson tagged him out too. We have seen a number of plays where a catcher made two putouts on the same play at the plate (where catchers belong). Wilson did it at third base.

COMMENT

Frazier was not the ideal player with whom to attempt a steal of home (even on a trick play). In his eight-year career, he stole *zero* bases, and attempted just one. Alston, for his part, was credited with both a stolen base and a caught stealing on the play. Wilson, the hustling catcher, once stole ten bases in a season (1958) without being caught. Which is as good an excuse as any to describe the strangest pinch-running performance in baseball history.

On June 15, 1974, the Orioles and White Sox were tied at 3 in the bottom of the ninth with one out and Elrod Hendricks on first. Earl Weaver sent in Don Baylor to run for the slow-footed Hendricks. With Brooks Robinson at the plate, on the first pitch Baylor took off for second. He was easily out but second baseman Ron Santo dropped the ball on the tag. The official scorer called it a caught stealing and an error on Santo. Buoyed by his good fortune, Baylor immediately stole third. Now 90 feet away from the walk-off win, and with dreams of glory, Baylor tried to steal home. Out. Yup, he was caught stealing twice in the inning (while also stealing a base).

Readers of a certain age may find it curious that Baylor would be used as a pinch-runner, much less be dashing around the bases helter skelter. The burly outfielder was known for getting hit by pitches deliberately (he led the league eight times, including 35 one year) because he was so big and strong that nothing hurt. In fact, though, he was fleet-footed as well: Baylor stole 20 or more bases in eight consecutive years, and once as many as 52. Then, at the age of 35, he abruptly stopped running, stealing just nine bases total in his last five seasons.

If Baylor's performance amounted to the worst base-running by a pinch-runner, the honor for worst base-running for an entire game belongs to the Giants' Robby Thompson. On June 27, 1986, in the fourth inning against the Reds, the rookie Thompson singled but was caught trying to steal second. In the sixth inning, same thing. In the ninth inning, with the game now tied at 6, Thompson led off with his third consecutive single. You guessed it, he tried to steal again. And was thrown out for the third time. The game remained tied in the eleventh inning when John Franco struck out Thompson. At least he couldn't get caught stealing again! Except the third strike got by the catcher, and Thompson reached first. Before he had a chance to try to steal for the fourth time, Franco picked him off. That goes down as a caught stealing, making Thompson the only player in major league history caught stealing four times in a game.

The alert reader may also scratch his head and wonder about *second baseman Ron Santo?* Santo was in the 15th and final year of his Hall of Fame career. In the first 14 years, all with the Cubs, he played just three games at second (and more than 2,000 at third). But when the Cubbies traded him cross-town to the White Sox in '74, the Sox played him quite a bit at second.

14: Three's a Crowd

On August 15, 1926, in the seventh inning of a game against the Boston Braves at Ebbets Field, with the bases loaded for the Robins, the legendary Babe Herman blasted a ball off the right field wall and raced to third with what he thought was a bases-clearing triple. However, he encountered *two* teammates already occupying the bag—Dazzy Vance, who started the play on second but got caught in a rundown between third and home and sought sanctuary at third; and Chick Fewster, who started the play on first and advanced to third without incident. (Herman, for his part, just blithely ran as far as he could without taking note of other base runners.) The Braves' second baseman, Doc Gautreau, retrieved the ball, tagged all three Dodgers and let the umpires sort things out. They correctly ruled that Vance, the lead runner, was entitled to the base, and Fewster and Herman were out. Yes, Herman doubled into a double-play.

COMMENT

The next day, the *New York Times'* article about the game included a delightfully terse explanation for the pile-on at third-base: "Vance was satisfied to advance one base on the blow, Fewster thought he ought to take two and Herman insisted on making three."[76] But the *Times* writer, Richard Vidmer, underrated the staying power of this play in baseball lore: "If it had been a more critical situation the Babe would wake up this morning and find himself famous."[77]

Vidmer did not mention a little-known fact about the play that adds texture: The third base coach, who surely screamed a lot of things at a lot of people as the play unfolded, was part-time catcher Mickey O'Neil. O'Neil replaced the usual third-base coach, Otto Miller, for that game for reasons never adequately explained. Maybe Miller sensed something crazy was on the horizon, and didn't want to be involved in an embarrassing part of baseball history for a second time: In 1920, he was tagged out by Bill Wambsganss for the final out of the only unassisted triple-play in World Series history. The closest I've come to an explanation for the Miller/O'Neil switch is a cryptic comment in an article about Dazzy Vance in the *Boston Globe* 35 years later: "Miller had complained that nothing ever happened at third."[78] If he said that, he was proven wrong!

The legend of the play grew over the decades. It was often said that Herman doubled into a *triple-play*, and Vance enjoyed telling people that Gautreau chased Herman all the way into right field to tag him for the third out. In that same *Globe* article, Gautreau is quoted as saying that "I've heard so many versions of that play I hardly know how it went myself, although I made both putouts." Meanwhile, Herman lamented that "if there was any justice, Vance would have been the one declared out because he's the one caused the traffic jam in the first place."[79] There's no justice in baseball, Babe.

13: Matthews' Mad Dash

In the tenth inning of the Cubs–Pirates game on June 29, 1985, the Pirates threatened to plate the winner. Doug Frobel was on second and Marvell Wynne on first with one out when Lee Mazzilli's base hit landed in front of Cubs left fielder Gary Matthews, who inadvertently kicked it toward the infield. Frobel, who held up thinking the ball might be caught, now raced home. Wynne, whose run was meaningless, raced to the plate as well, almost overtaking Frobel. Matthews, sprinting in from the outfield after retrieving the ball, ended up in the infield in hot pursuit of the two Pirates. It resembled a track event, with three runners nearing the finish line in close proximity. If Matthews tagged Wynne before Frobel reached the plate, the inning would be over. Inexplicably, Matthews ignored Wynne, running past him in pursuit of Frobel. But his approach worked. Matthews halted his advance ten feet short of the plate and flipped the ball to catcher Jody Davis who tagged Frobel for the out.

COMMENT

The Cubs lost anyway (on a walk-off home run by Tony Pena), but it took 15 innings. The Matthews play is one of four in our list involving an outfielder giving a ball a big boot, thus indirectly raising this question: Who is the best soccer player in baseball history? A number of major leaguers crossed over to play professional football and basketball, and countless players starred in all three in high school or even college. A surprising number of major leaguers also played high-level hockey. But soccer? One rarely hears about a soccer/baseball combo.

One exception is Jimmie Wilson, a superb catcher in the 1920s and '30s who played professional soccer before turning to the diamond. A more recent exception is Curtis Pride, a utility player from 1993 to 2006. While in high school, Pride was named one of the top 15 youth soccer prospects in the world. In 1986, *Parade* named him a High School soccer All American. Here's something else about Pride: He's deaf, one of just a handful of deaf players in major league history. By far the most successful, William Hoy (insensitively nicknamed "Dummy"), batted .288 over 14 seasons and scored 100 runs or more nine times. Hoy was a superb center fielder who once threw out three runners at home in a game, a record that has been equaled but never surpassed. The catcher who made the putouts? The legendary Connie Mack.

 # 12: I Don't Know? He's on Third.

This play, which took place in a Giants–Dodgers game on October 3, 1916, is the single play in the 150 Most Bizarre Plays which I neither saw nor read a description by a first-hand observer. Besides the box score, the only record of it I can find is its mention in J.P. Hoornstra's fine book about Dodgers history. Specifically, the book mentions a "1–3–6–2–8–2 double-play featuring a crazy run down between third and home."[80] The beauty of box scores and official scoring is that, in combination, they often tell you what you need to know. Here, in the first inning the Giants had runners on first and third and Dave Robertson laid down a bunt. The pitcher, Sherry Smith, fielded it and threw to first baseman Jake Daubert for one out, and Daubert threw to the shortstop, Ivy Olson, who was covering second, but too late to catch Dave Robertson. The runner from third, Buck Herzog, broke for the plate, but Olson's throw home beat him there and caused Herzog to scramble back to third. Now things get interesting, as the catcher, Otto Miller, threw to Hy Myers, the center fielder (!), who had alertly raced in to cover third. (The third baseman, Mike Mowrey, presumably came down the line to field the bunt, and never made it back to third, and the shortstop Olson remained at second.) Myers raced Herzog back toward home and threw to Miller who tagged Herzog out for the only 1–3–6–2–8–2 play in baseball history, with Myers recording perhaps the strangest outfield assist in baseball history.

COMMENT

The left fielder getting involved at third base would be odd enough, but understandable. The *center fielder*? According to Hoornstra, on the very next play Meyers "lost a fly ball in the sun for an inside-the-park two run homer." (The box score indicates that the recipient of this good fortune was Art Fletcher, whose fluky home run was the Giants' only extra base hit in the game. They hit 10 singles.) Yep, Myers raced in from the outfield all the way to third base for a put out to help prevent a run and, on the next play, couldn't find a ball that may have been just a few feet from him, resulting in two runs. In case those back-to-back plays don't qualify this inning as one of the strangest ever, let's back up. On all three plays preceding the twilight zone double-play and inside-the-parker, the Dodgers committed errors. And here is Hoornstra's description of what happened in the fifth inning after the Dodgers stole a base because the pitcher inexplicably wound up: "That's when [Giants manager John] McGraw decided he had seen enough. He left. McGraw left the dugout. Then Ebbets Field. Then the borough of Brooklyn. Then the state of New York. He went all the way to the Laurel Park racetrack in Maryland to play the ponies rather than manage the final two games of the season."

As long as we're lingering on the box score of that incredible game, there is another nugget to consider. Each team sent up one pinch-hitter that day, and each pinch-hitter reached safely: for the Giants, the legendary Casey Stengel; for the Dodgers, the legendary Hans Lobert (who raced a horse to a virtual draw).

11: Ricky's Recovery

On August 7, 2001, with the game tied in the bottom of the ninth at Wrigley Field against the Rockies, the Cubs had runners on first and second with one out when Joe Girardi's single into left field seemed destined to end the game. The speedy Ricky Gutierrez rounded third and headed home until he stumbled and fell on his face. He managed to scramble to his feet and retreat safely to third, but his change of plans wrecked the whole party. Sammy Sosa, who started the play at first and was headed for third when Gutierrez fell, now raced back to second, making it ahead of catcher Sal Fasano's throw to shortstop Juan Uribe. But all the improvising left Girardi out to dry between first and second. In the ensuing rundown, several Rockies touched the ball, always with a wary eye on Gutierrez, who kept faking a run home. Todd Helton chased Girardi backed to second, where Sosa already stood, but before tagging Girardi, Helton turned back to gauge Gutierrez's progress. When he did so, Girardi raced back toward first. Helton tossed the ball to pitcher Gabe White, covering first, who tagged Girardi out, but not before Gutierrez took off and beat the throw home by a hair. Game over. Gutierrez, who started the chaos with a face plant, ended up scoring the game-winning run.

COMMENT

Something was in the air that day. Home plate umpire Angel Hernandez ejected a professional football player high up in the stands. Say what? Hernandez made a questionable call in the sixth inning that cost the Cubs a run. When former Chicago Bears defensive tackle Steve "Mongo" McMichael took the mike in the announcers' booth to sing "Take Me Out to the Ballgame" during the seventh inning stretch, he first said to the crowd, "I'm going to have to have a talk with that umpire down there." Hernandez signaled McMichael's ejection, and supposedly asked crew chief Randy Marsh to call to the press box to have McMichael removed. McMichael finished singing first.

McMichael was not the only non-player ever ejected from a game. On August 23, 1989, the Expos' mascot Youppi got the heave-ho for laying atop the Dodgers' dugout and annoying Tommy LaSorda. Poor Youppi was tossed in the seventh inning of a scoreless tie. Little did he know he would hang out in the clubhouse, or wherever ejected mascots hang out, for 15 more innings. That's right, the Expos and Dodgers played 22 scoreless innings until Rick Dempsey homered against Dennis Martinez, who was in relief for the only time that year. (He started 33 games. From 1987 through 1997, he started 299 games and pitched in relief twice.) Until Dempsey's blow, the Dodgers banged out 19 hits without scoring a run. That would have shattered the previous record of hits in a shutout (14) but Dempsey spoiled the fun. For their part, the Expos banged out 13 hits, falling one short of the record. The combined 32 hits in the game included none by the shortstops: Alfredo Griffin and Spike Owen combined to go for 0–17. The six Expos pitchers combined for 22 innings without issuing a walk.

10: A Long Way Home

On June 6, 1976, in the seventh inning the Phillies had Greg Luzinski on second and Dick Allen on first with one out when Jay Johnstone laced a line-drive single to center off John Montefusco. Giants centerfielder Larry Herndon played the ball on one bounce, then sprinted into the infield hoping to make a miraculous force play at second. (Both the second baseman and shortstop went for the catch and were not close to the base.) However, Allen beat Herndon to the bag. Herndon noticed that Luzinski had rounded third so he kept up his mad dash toward the transfixed bull. He actually tagged Luzinski out for what should have been unprecedented: an unassisted put-out by an outfielder of a player between third and home. Except Herndon dropped the ball and Luzinski scrambled home safely. Instead of making history, Herndon merely made an error.

COMMENT

Three of the players involved in this doozy were among the most colorful and/or controversial personalities ever to grace the diamond. Johnstone was a famous prankster who enjoyed setting teammates' cleats on fire and the like. His books, tellingly titled, *Temporary Insanity*, *Over the Edge*, and *Some of My Best Friends Are Crazy*, include hundreds of pages of such shenanigans.

The year before Mark Fidrych dazzled the baseball world, the National League experienced a less famous version of him: John

"Count" Montefusco. The Count was very good—he won 16 games and Rookie of the Year—and liked to say so. He made outrageous predictions ("I'm going to shut out the Dodgers"), then made good on them. But like Fidrych, he spent the rest of his injury-plagued career trying to re-bottle the rookie magic. After his glorious first year, Montefusco kicked around for ten more seasons in which he lost exactly as many games (72) as he won.

Dick Allen brought controversy with him wherever he went (which was to six teams, in part for that very reason), but no one denied his prodigious talent. While known for tape-measure home runs, Allen was the first player in the modern era to hit two inside-the-park home runs in the same game. Bill James rates him the second most controversial player of all-time (behind Rogers Hornsby), though surely much of the controversy stemmed from Allen being a black man who did not suffer indignities quietly in an era where the baseball establishment did not accept brazenness from blacks. Allen, who passed away on December 7, 2020, may well be the best player not in the Hall of Fame.

In the game featuring Herndon's mad dash, the non-controversial Jim Kaat pitched a complete game victory while banging out three hits and driving in three runs.

9: *The Nearer Your Destination…*

On August 16, 2003, in the Yankees–Orioles games, Jack Cust was on second base in the twelfth inning with the Birds down a run. Larry Bigbie's gapper should have scored Cust easily, but halfway between third and home Cust slipped and fell flat on his back. When he got up, he found himself in a run-down, a dead duck. Somehow the Yankees screwed up and left home plate untended, so Cust triumphantly sprinted home with the dramatic game-tying run … except on the way home he fell on his face. Was tagged out. Game over.

COMMENT

Who tagged Cust to complete the wacky play and end the game? Huge hint: Just two months later, this player also ended perhaps the greatest game of all-time. That would be Aaron Boone who, on October 18, 2003, hit the eleventh-inning walk-off home run in Game 7 of the 2003 American League Championship, sending the Yankees to the World Series and extending the 85 year Red Sox curse.

In a sport full of strange career arcs, Boone had one of the strangest. The Game 7 home run was the most famous in the history of baseball's most dominant franchise. (Note to Reggie Jackson and Bucky Dent fans: Feel free to disagree.) Needless to say, it made Boone a hero in the Big Apple. But, although Boone was just 30 years old and in his prime, the heroic homer was his last plate appearance in a Yankees uniform. During the off-season, less than three months after his storied home run, Boone tore the anterior cruciate ligament in his left knee during a pick-up basketball game. A month later, the Yankees, that most sentimental of franchises, released him. After sitting out the 2004 season while rehabbing his knee, Boone came back to play with three teams over five undistinguished seasons before calling it quits.

Boone exemplifies a riches-to-rags career arc more common in baseball than any sport. An even more extreme example is Red Sox pitcher Bill Rohr. In his debut, the 22-year-old right-hander out-pitched Whitey Ford in Yankee Stadium. More importantly, he was one out (indeed one strike) away from a no-hitter—Elston Howard broke up the no-no and Rohr's heart with a bloop single in the ninth inning. Still, a one-hit shutout is close to the greatest pitching debut of all-time. Of course, anyone can pitch *one* great game. In Rohr's next start, several days later at Fenway Park, the Yankees had their chance for revenge. The Sox won 6–1 behind Rohr's second consecutive dominant performance. At that point, Red Sox nation was giddy about the rookie sensation. Rohr won a total of one more game, finishing his career 3–3 with an ERA of 5.64.

One other crazy career arc marks one of the saddest stories in baseball history. As everyone knows, seven White Sox players accepted money in exchange for throwing the 1919 World Series. An eighth, Buck Weaver, received no money and apparently played hard, but was thrown out of baseball along with his more culpable teammates because he knew about the bribe and did not come forward to expose it. In modern tellings of the story, Weaver is presented as, if not the hero, at least the innocent persecuted victim. His desperate letter appealing to be reinstated to baseball enjoys a prominent display in the Hall of Fame in Cooperstown.

There was a truer hero and more innocent victim on that White Sox team. Rookie pitcher Dickey Kerr had such a reputation for honesty that the gamblers never approached him. Kerr did not know about the fix, and almost thwarted it—he pitched a three-hit shutout in Game 3 and a ten-inning complete game in Game 6. The next two seasons, Kerr won 21 and 19 games. Having won 53 games and two World Series games over his first three seasons, Kerr asked for a salary of $3,500. The notoriously cheap White Sox owner, Charles Comiskey, declined. An embittered Kerr quit the majors at the age of 28. (He came back for a cup of coffee in 1925.)

8: Heads-Up Triple-Play

On September 7, 1935, in the ninth inning the Red Sox, trailing 5–3, loaded the bases with nobody out, and Joe Cronin hit a screaming line drive right at Indians third-baseman Odell Hale. The ball was struck so hard that Hale couldn't get his glove up: It bounced off his forehead into the air, and sent Red Sox runners in motion all over the diamond. However, the ball hit Hale so hard that it caromed all the way to shortstop Bill Knickerbocker, who snagged it before it hit the ground. Knickerbocker threw to second baseman Roy Hughes, who stepped on second and threw to first baseman Hal Trosky for the game-ending triple-play—started by the third baseman's face.

COMMENT

The cursed Red Sox suffered as unlucky an ending as one can imagine. But seeing as it was the first game of a double-header, they had a chance to soothe the pain with a victory in the second game. They fell 5–4, leaving two runners stranded in the ninth. Oral Hildebrand pitched the ninth to notch his second save of the season. His first came in the opening game of the double-header. He had none from April through September 6, and two on September 7.

It doesn't make our list bizarre plays, because it wasn't in the major leagues, but on July 1911, in a Pacific Coast League game, Walter Carlisle made what is likely the only unassisted triple-play by an *outfielder* in professional baseball history. Playing shallow with the game tied in the sixth inning and runners on first and second, Carlisle made a somersault catch on a line drive, then raced to step on second and tag the runner who started on first. The play was no fluke: Carlisle had been a circus acrobat.[81]

Carlisle's immortality occurred three years after his rather forgettable stint in the big leagues. When the Red Sox acquired him from the Los Angeles Angels in the Pacific Coast League in 1907, they were believed to have acquired a player who could do everything and play almost any position. The next year the Red Sox brought up the bright prospect. Carlisle had one base hit in ten at-bats before being returned to the minors, where he remained for another 13 years before retiring at the age of 41.

7: *The Old Two Balls in One Play Trick*

You may have heard of the legendary potato play. (If not, you will soon.) That is not included in the 150 Most Bizarre Plays because it was in a minor league game. But, incredibly, on June 30, 1959, a major league game featured something oddly similar and far more involved. In the fourth inning, with the Cardinals leading the Cubs 4–1, Stan Musial took ball four and sprinted to first when the wild pitch sailed past the catcher to the backstop. The pitcher (Bob Anderson) and catcher (Sammy Taylor) protested that the pitch had grazed Musial's bat, and while they argued at the plate, Musial rounded first and headed for second. Third baseman Alvin Dark streaked to the backstop to retrieve the ball, but before he arrived, the bat boy, thinking it was a foul ball, picked it up and tossed it to field announcer Pat Pieper. Pieper, realizing it was a live ball, let it drop to his feet. Dark grabbed the ball and threw to shortstop Ernie Banks to try and nail Musial at second.

As all this was happening, the home plate umpire, Vic Delmore, foolishly handed a new ball to catcher Taylor. The pitcher, Anderson, seeing Musial race towards second, grabbed the ball from Taylor and fired the second ball in the direction of second base. Dark's throw arrived too late to get Musial, and Anderson's throw sailed into center field. Musial instinctively headed for third, but Banks chased him down and tagged him out with the original ball. The umpires huddled and decided that Musial was indeed out.

Comment

The comic screw-up didn't affect the game (won by the Cards 4–1) but it may have had serious consequences. After the season, National League president Warren Giles fired umpire Delmore. Delmore died of a heart attack several months later.

As for the potato play, catcher Dave Bresnahan (the great-nephew of Hall of Fame catcher Roger Bresnahan) threw a peeled potato into left field, luring an unsuspecting runner to race home where Bresnahan was waiting to tag him out with the actual ball. (The umpires disallowed the play and allowed the run to score.) It happened August 31, 1987, in a Class-A game in Williamsport, Pennsylvania. The play continues to live in lore. On its one-year anniversary, Williamsport retired Bresnahan's uniform, No. 59. Fans bringing a potato were admitted for one dollar. The game sold out. To commemorate the tenth anniversary in 1997, Ira Berkow wrote about the play in the *New York Times*. Bresnahan defended the play to Berkow: "The rule book doesn't say anything about not throwing a potato in a game," he insisted.[82]

As for the Musial play in 1959, note the role played by "field announcer, Pat Pieper." In the old days, the public address announcer used to stand on the field near the backstop. Until 1932, when the Cubs installed an electronic system, Pieper used to run up and down foul territory with his 14-pound megaphone bellowing announcements to the crowd.

 # 6: Reverse Logic

On April 19, 2013, the craziness started in the eighth inning, with the Brewers seeking to extend their 5–4 lead over the Cubs. Jean Segura singled and stole second. After Ryan Braun walked, Segura tried to steal third. However, he left too soon—before the Cubs' pitcher, Shawn Camp, stepped toward home. Camp threw the ball to the third baseman, Luis Valbuena, essentially picking off Segura. Segura got in a run down, and ended up back at second, where he had company: Braun had arrived. Valbuena tagged them both. Segura was the one entitled to the base; Braun was out. But Segura decided *he* was out, and headed for the dugout. The first base coach, Garth Iorg, alertly screamed to Segura to find a safe haven at first base. Second baseman Darwin Barney grabbed the ball out of Valbuena's glove and chased Segura. But Segura reached first ahead of him. Moments later, Segura, apparently dazed over having started the play at second and ended up at first, *again* headed for the dugout. Iorg intercepted him and returned him to first. The umpires ruled that Segura was entitled to stay there. He started the play on second and ended up back at first, having essentially stolen first base.

COMMENT

Naturally, Segura was not overjoyed with this backward movement, so on the next pitch he tried to re-steal second. He was thrown out to end the inning. Segura attempted three steals in the inning. One was successful, one was unsuccessful, and the third is hard to judge. He was, after all, safe, but his teammate was out and he (Segura) lost a base on the play.

In the ninth inning, still trailing by a run, with two outs and the bases empty, the Cubs' Dioner Navarro singled to keep hope alive. Pinch-runner Julio Borbon no doubt sensed that there was only one fitting way for this game to end: Yes, he was caught stealing. On the season, it was the only time Borbon was caught (out of eight attempts).

Early in the twentieth century, several players *deliberately* stole first base from second—trying to draw a throw so the runner on third could sprint home. The most reported effort of this sort was by the Senators' Germany Schaefer. As we have seen, Schaefer once ran the bases in reverse, i.e., from first to home to third to second. He was apparently accustomed to running in the wrong direction. In the bottom of the ninth inning of a tie game against the White Sox in 1911, Schaefer was on first in the ninth inning with the winning run on third. He stole second, hoping to draw a throw, but the Sox let him go unimpeded. So Schaefer proceeded to run back to first on the next pitch. While the White Sox players protested, Schaefer headed back toward second, creating a rundown, during which his teammate, Clyde Millan, sprinted home. Unfortunately, Milan was thrown out.

That, at any rate, is the conventional account which has been repeated in dozens of publications. In *The Glory of Their Times*, Schafer's teammate, Davey Jones, tells a similar story but with the details changed: The game was 1908, the opponent Cleveland, the runner on third was Jones. In Jones' telling, the play worked better: Schaefer was safe at second and Jones scored.[83]

Of course, there is nothing necessarily inconsistent about the two tales. Perhaps Schaefer stole first in both 1908 and 1911. It is fun to think that the play was simply part of his base-running arsenal. Regardless, a subsequent MLB rule change eliminates the possibility of the intentional steal of first base. It stipulates that a runner is out who "runs the bases in reverse order for the purpose of confusing the defense or making a travesty of the game."

Note that Jean Segura lacked the requisite evil intent (he ended up at first seeking sanctuary, not to confuse the defense or mock the game). Thus, the umpires had a legitimate basis for allowing him to remain at first. *Except*, as we have seen, a coach is not allowed to give a player a physical assist. Garth Iorg's interception of Segura should have resulted in him being called out. Even apart from that, the league office declared that Segura should not have been allowed to return to first: The rule forbidding a player from reaching a base after "abandoning the effort" at base-running should have been applied and Segura called out.

5: *There's a Catch*

On July 27, 2009, with a runner on second in the second inning, the Giants' Randy Winn lined a ball that reached Pirates right fielder Garrett Jones on a fly. However, the ball glanced off Jones' glove, then his shin, followed by his foot, which inadvertently punted the ball back towards the infield. Second baseman Delwyn Young, moving to shallow right on the play, saw the ball (on its way back) flying by, and made a spectacular, diving bare-hand grab. Apparently not believing what he had seen, umpire Dale Scott ruled base hit, though the ball clearly never touched ground. Despite the missed call, the Pirates retired Winn, who could not believe his eyes either and was tagged out while meandering between first and second. But the umpire's error meant a run scored on the play. It also meant that the craziest catch in baseball history went down as a single.

COMMENT

Wouldn't it have been something if the gifted base hit allowed Winn to hit .300 on the season? Alas, he had an off-year and batted just .262. But two seasons earlier, Winn did indeed hit .300 on the nose. (Actually .3001686.) He came into the last game of the season batting .299. After his first-inning double, manager Bruce Bochte pulled him from the game to preserve the achievement.

Here is another quirky trivia question: Which of the participants in this play became a Hall of Famer? That would be Dale Scott, the first openly gay umpire in major league history and a 2015 inductee into the National Gay and Lesbian Hall of Fame. At this writing the only living major leaguer to come out is Billy Bean, not to be confused (though he often is) with Billy Beane, the long-time A's general manager made famous by *Moneyball*.

4: Can't Tell the Players Without a Scorecard

On April 17, 1993, the Angels led the Orioles 6–5 in the eighth inning, and had the bases loaded with one out. Jeff Tackett was on third, Brady Anderson second, and Chito Martinez first, with Mike Devereaux batting against Joe Grahe. Devereaux looped a fly to shallow left-center, and center-fielder Chad Curtis gave pursuit and attempted a catch. The short version of what happened thereafter is that anarchy broke out: An array of Angels and Orioles ran around the infield in all directions. For a more specific description, I'm turning it over to *Los Angeles Times* writer Bob Nightengale, for two reasons. First, it is not possible to improve on his version. Second, for anyone who does not understand what happened (that will be most of you), there will be someone else to blame besides me.

> Curtis dove for the ball and ... well ... who knows? Curtis said he caught it.... Umpire Ted Hendry ruled he trapped it....
>
> Curtis hit the cutoff man, Snow, who was under the assumption that Curtis caught the ball. He figured Tackett had already scored, and was throwing to Gonzales at third to tag out Anderson.
>
> Gonzales, who had only to touch third for the force on Anderson, instead threw the ball to Orton. Likewise, Orton needed only to touch home for the force on Tackett, but he ran toward third base where everyone was standing....

Orton kept running, and before he knew it tagged Tackett, Anderson, Martinez ... [for] an 8–3–5–2 double-play.[84]

COMMENT

Earlier we encountered the famous play in which Babe Herman doubled into a double-play, which also resulted in three runners at third base. This play had three runners at third, and an additional runner at second! Curtis, the man whose non-catch created all the confusion, said "I was out there counting up the outs, and I came up with four."[85] Other post-game comments by the participants were equally odd. While the third base coach Ferraro and Pitcher Grahe acknowledged that they were screaming at their various teammates, Angels manager Buck Martinez said, "I wasn't yelling anything because I didn't know what was going on."[86]

Brady Anderson, one of the Orioles running in circles, had a strange career. In 1996, at the age of 32 and in his ninth year in the big leagues, he transformed himself from a speedy center-fielder with modest power to a super slugger. His previous high in home runs was 21, but in '96 he hit 50. For good measure, this lifetime .250 hitter batted .297. The next season, Anderson regressed dramatically to 18 homers while batting .288, and the season after that plummeted to .236 while again hitting 18 home runs.

Since this was the steroids era, it was widely assumed that in '96 Anderson received external assistance. But that season was neither the first nor last in which his performance skyrocketed. In his first four years in the league, he never hit higher than .231 and managed a total of 11 home runs in 1,166 at-bats. In 1992, he blossomed, batting .271 and slugging 21 homers. Still, that was within the range of normal for a coming-of-age season by a 28-year-old. There was modest regression over the next three years, then the explosion in '96, followed by another regression. Then, in 1999, at the age of 35, Anderson had the second-best season of his 15-year career. He batted .282, 56 points higher than the previous season, slugged 24 homers, easily his best except for the 50 home run explosion, and his .404 on-base percentage was a career best. For good measure, he stole 36 bases, by far his best output in seven years. Anderson declined modestly the next year, and in 2001 nose-dived to .202 with just eight home runs in 501 at-bats.

Baseball history is full of one-season wonders, as well as players who enjoyed several exemplary seasons followed by a sharp drop. There are also examples of every other conceivable permutation. But three standout seasons scattered over 15 years? Steroids may explain Brady Anderson's incredible outlier year, but the full zigzaggy career arc defies ready explanation.

3: *There's No Crying in Baseball*

On July 9, 1985, in a game between the Blue Jays and Mariners, in the bottom of the third inning the Mariners' Phil Bradley was on second base when Gorman Thomas singled. Bradley tried to score but was cut down by Jesse Barfield's throw to catcher Buck Martinez. (That's the same Buck Martinez who was involved in the previous play as a manager.) However, the collision at the plate broke Martinez's ankle. Thomas, seeing Martinez writhing in agony, raced for third. From a seated position, Martinez threw to third baseman Garth Iorg to try and nab Thomas. But the throw was wild (understandably) and ended up in left field. Thomas streaked home, while left fielder George Bell retrieved the ball and threw it home. Martinez, still on the ground in agony, nevertheless caught the ball and tagged out Thomas. As we have seen, a number of catchers recorded two putouts on the same play. Only Martinez did so with a broken ankle.

COMMENT

Thomas is one of only a few players directly involved in three of our 150 Most Bizarre Plays. Weirdly, he played the same odd role in two of them—the second player caught at the plate on one play. Coincidence? Maybe not. On this play he inexplicably slowed up as he approached the plate. Perhaps taking mercy on an obviously injured catcher? Maybe just a guy with bad base-running instincts.

Iorg and Martinez, meanwhile, were both participants in two top five plays. Martinez also makes a cameo appearance in *Ball Four*. He is in the opposing lineup as Jim Bouton's Mariners discuss at a pre-game meeting how to pitch each batter. No one knows anything about the rookie Martinez. The inimitable manager, Joe Shultz, declares that, under the circumstances, "we'll just zitz em."[87]

2: Can't Wynn for Losing

In the first inning against the Pirates on June 19, 1974, the Dodgers had the bases loaded—Lee Lacy on third, Jimmy Wynn on second, and Ron Cey at first. Joe Ferguson worked a 3–2 count against Jerry Reuss. The payoff pitch seemed like strike three, in part because the home plate umpire, Dave Davidson, started to raise his arm before changing his mind. The only person on the field who realized it was ball four was Wynn. While the Pirates started to leave the field, as did Lacy (instead of trotting home), Wynn sped around third and scored. Thanks to Wynn's mad dash, Lacy and the Pirates realized what was happening. Reuss raced to the mound where catcher Manny Sanguillen had rolled the ball (as used to be done on inning-ending strikeouts) and Sanguillen returned to the plate whereas Lacy also took off for the plate (starting from way outside the base line, as he had almost reached the Dodgers' dugout). Reuss threw to Sanguillen just in time to tag out a sliding Lacy. After much confusion, umpire-in-chief Ed Sudol ruled Lacy safe (and thus a run scored) and Wynn out for passing Lacy. Lacy was entitled to an automatic advance on the walk, whereas Wynn was entitled to nothing despite being the most alert player on the field.

COMMENT

Wait a minute. Wynn passed Lacy before Lacy touched the plate. That means the run scored *after* the third out. Is that even a thing? Sudol defended the decision to count the run, saying it comported with "common sense" and the rule book does not cover this situation.[88] He clarified that Lacy would have been declared out had he entered the Dodgers' dugout, which some observers claim he did. But Lacy denied that he made it into the dugout, and none of the umpires saw him do so.

There was a certain logic to Sanguillen's role in the play: He assumed the pitch was a called strike because he didn't much believe in walks. Sanguillen was the only player since 1900 with at least six straight seasons with 475 plate appearances and fewer than 22 walks. This admittedly contrived statistic conveys a truth: Sanguillen rarely walked. In 1973, he walked just 17 times in 619 plate appearances, which is borderline ridiculous. In the post-season, Sanguillen got *really* impatient: In 104 plate appearances, spanning six post-seasons, he walked exactly once. On the bright side, the notorious bad-ball hitter somehow rarely struck out—only twice more than 40 times in a season and never 50.

1: *Hockey Game Breaks Out*

On September 22, 1974, just three months after the previous play, the Cardinals and Cubs were deadlocked at 5 in the ninth inning. The Cards Al "Mad Hungarian" Hrabosky was pitching to Bill Matlock. Matlock did not appreciate Hrabosky's manic dance behind the mound between pitches. Whenever Hrabosky made it back to the mound, Matlock stepped out of the batter's box and retreated to the on-deck circle. This charade so infuriated umpire Shag Crawford that he pursued Matlock to demand his return to the batter's box, and this so infuriated Cubs manager Jim Marshall that he charged out of the dugout to back up his player. For some reason, the on-deck hitter, Jose Cardenal, accompanied Marshall, ensuring that Crawford heard two earfuls of angry protest as he returned to his position behind the plate.

With those two chirping at him, and manager Marshall the only participant actually in the batter's box (though obviously without a bat), Crawford ordered Hrabosky to pitch. Hrabosky obeyed, and, though the pitch was clearly high, Crawford called a strike. Now Cardenal screamed at Matlock to get back in the box so as not to give away the at-bat, but didn't wait for Matlock to comply: He moved into the batter's box himself lest it remain unoccupied. Matlock was not about to be usurped by the on-deck hitter, so he raced to join Cardenal in the batter's box. With both batters in the box, bats cocked, and manager Marshall just to the other side of catcher Ted Simmons, Crawford inexplicably ordered Hrabosky to throw another pitch toward the scrum. This he did, and it almost hit Matlock. Words were exchanged, Simmons punched Matlock in the face, Cardenal punched Simmons, and the benches emptied.

COMMENT

One of Crawford's sons, Joey, was a leading NBA official known for anger management issues. (He once challenged Tim Duncan to a fight, and once ejected Duncan for laughing.) But Joey, perhaps a chip off the old block, never officiated a play quite as oddly as his dad did this one. Amazingly, the only person Crawford ejected was manager Marshall. Players threw punches and trespassed on the batter's box, and Crawford ejected a manager for arguing.

In attendance was the widow of Dizzy Dean, invited to the game as part of a ceremony in which the Cardinals retired Dean's uniform number. Patricia Dean claimed to enjoy the strange happenings at home plate and the resulting brawl. "They must have done this for Diz," she told reporters. "It looked like the old Gashouse Gang."[89]

Conclusion

What are we to make of the fact that our top two plays both occurred in 1974? At least in the hands of astrologists that might not be pure coincidence. And it was the summer of Watergate and Nixon's resignation. We cannot put it past some creative historian to make a connection.

Speaking of creative constructions, consider the comment attached to Play # 12: "On the very next play [Hy] Meyers 'lost a fly ball in the sun for an inside-the-park two run homer.'" I'd love to see that play. Or at least read a description from someone who saw it. What was Meyers doing—running around flailing? Covering his head? Did his fellow outfielders race over and try to rescue him? The play might have merited inclusion in our list of the most bizarre plays if only we knew more. In which case, we would have had *back-to-back* plays making the list, both involving Hy Myers. (In Play # 12, Myers sprinted to the infield to help pull off a 1–3–6–2–8–2 out.)

Now consider Play # 149, where the same Hy Myers grounded into a double play with the help of the shortstop's ankle. That play took place during Game 1 of the World Series, on October 7, 1916, just four days after Play #12. So that single week witnessed perhaps the strangest sequence of back-to-back plays in baseball history and a play the *Washington Post* declared "has probably never occurred on any ball grounds."

Was something in the air during the first week of October 1916? (And what in the world is it about this Hy Myers guy?) Of course, we can unearth meaningful or quirky world and sports news that took place on October 3 (thousands of workers went on strike against Standard Oil) and October 7 (Georgia Tech defeated Cumberland College 222–0, still the biggest blowout in college football history), but we could do that for every week. Only the flimsiest magical thinker would read anything into these events coinciding with exceptionally bizarre baseball.

One could argue that the entire 1916 World Series, featuring the Red Sox and Robins, has a special place in baseball lore. Game 1, which featured Myers' freakish double-play, came down to a dramatic ninth inning in which the Robins scored four runs to make the game 6–5, and loaded the bases. Carl Mays (the only man in baseball history to throw a fatal pitch) got the final out with none other than Fred Merkel representing the winning run at second. Game 2 featured a pitching duel for the ages. Both starting pitchers, Babe Ruth and Sherry Smith, went the 14-inning distance, with the Red Sox prevailing 2–1. The only run yielded by Ruth was a first-inning inside-the-park home-run by, who else, Hy Myers. Though Smith was almost as brilliant as Ruth, he managed only two strikeouts in the 14 innings—both Ruth himself.

Game 3 produced the third consecutive one-run game, and the only Robins win. The headhunter, Carl Mays, lost the game but hit only one Robins batter. You guessed it: Hy Myers. The Red Sox won Game 4 decisively, 6–2. Larry Gardner, who never hit more than four home runs in a season in his 17-year career, hit his second in two days. In Game 5, the Sox put away the series with a 4–1 win behind Ernie Shore's three-hitter. The leading hitter in the series for the Robins was a young outfielder named Casey Stengel.

It is kind of mind-blowing to think of Ruth pitching to Stengel. Ruth seems like a (or *the*) player from the game's ancient days, and Stengel an almost modern figure. Casey managed Tug McGraw, who was still pitching when Roger Clemens entered the league. Clemens faced Albert Pujols. And so the game passes down through the generations, never growing old. But notwithstanding the Ruth–Stengel match-up, and all the drama, in truth the 1916 World Series was no more (or less) historical than most. Inspect any series and you are likely to find all sorts of nuggets.

So, to return to the question that sparked this digression, there is really no explanation for why the first week in October is overrepresented in the collection of the most bizarre plays in baseball history. It was a cool week, like every week in baseball. Revisiting the game's past helps us stay young.

Notes

Preface

1. Ty Cobb with Al Stump, *My Life in Baseball: The True Record* (Lincoln: University of Nebraska Press, 1993), 126.
2. *Ibid.*
3. Tim Kurkjian, *Is This a Great Game or What? From A-Rod's Heart to Zim's Head* (New York: St. Martin's, 2007), 60.

The Plays

1. Stanley Milliken, "First Victory Moves Bookmakers to Increase Odds on Chances of Boston Team," *Washington Post* (October 8, 1916), S-1.
2. Bill Deane, *Finding the Hidden-Ball Trick: The Colorful History of Baseball's Oldest Ruse* (Lanham, MD: Rowman & Littlefield, 2015), 5.
3. Allen Barra, *Clearing the Bases: The Greatest Baseball Debates of the Last Century* (Lincoln: University of Nebraska Press, 2002), 176–79.
4. Jayson Stark, *The Stark Truth: The Most Overrated & Underrated Players in Baseball History* (Chicago: Triumph Books, 2007), 157.
5. Harold Kaese, "Sox Lose Dignity, Possibly Siebert, and All Hopes," *Boston Globe*, August 8, 1971, 77.
6. *Ibid.*
7. "'Weirdest Play' Helps Dodgers Nudge Pirates," *Washington Post*, May 24, 1966, D-1.
8. John Rosengren, *The Fight of Their Lives: How Juan Marichal and John Roseboro Turned Baseball's Ugliest Brawl into a Story of Forgiveness and Redemption*

(Guilford, CT: Globe Pequot Press, 2014). See especially Chapter 5.
9. Tom Callahan, *Gods at Play: An Eyewitness Account of Great Moments in American Sports* (New York: W.W. Norton, 2020), 68.
10. Michael Lewis, *Moneyball: The Art of Winning an Unfair Game* (New York: W.W. Norton, 2004), 19.
11. Harvey Frommer, *Baseball's Greatest Managers* (Guilford, CT: Lyons Press, 1985), 217.
12. Grant Brisbee, "In Search of Baseball's Dumbest Rule," SBNation, August 2, 2013, https://www.sbnation.com/2013/8/2/4583006/baseball-dumbest-rule-robby-thompson-mariners.
13. Joshua Prager, *The Echoing Green: The Untold Story of Bobby Thomson, Ralph Branca and the Shot Heard Round the World* (New York: Vintage, 2008), 394.
14. Joe Posnanski, "Flipping Out," NBC Sportsworld, https://sportsworld.nbcsports.com/blue-jays-rangers-seventh-inning-jose-bautista-bat-flip-russell-martin-throw/.
15. "Six Players in Triple-Play," *New York Times*, May 17, 1913: 9.
16. Ray Istorico, *Greatness in Waiting: An Illustrated History of the Early New York Yankees, 1903–1919* (Jefferson, NC: McFarland, 2013), 189.
17. Daniel Okrent and Steve Wulf, *Baseball Anecdotes* (New York: Oxford University Press, 1989), 217.
18. Joe Posnanski, "10 Questions About the New Intentional Walk Rule," MLB.com, March 3, 2017, https://www.

Notes

mlb.com/news/questions-about-the-new-intentional-walk-rule-c217773876.

19. Lawrence Ritter, *The Glory of Their Times: The Story of the Early Days of Baseball Told by the Men Who Played It* (New York: Perennial, 2002), 241.

20. Nicholas Dawidoff, *The Catcher Was a Spy: The Mysterious Life of Moe Berg* (New York: Vintage, 1995).

21. Ritter, *The Glory of Their Times*, 213.

22. "Gharrity's Homer Retires His Side," *New York Times*, September 12, 1920, A22.

23. David Vincent, *Home Runs Most Wanted: The Top Ten Book of Monumental Dingers, Prodigious Swingers, and Everything Long-Ball* (Dulles, VA: Potomac Books, 2009), 19.

24. Michael Kelly, "Harrison's 4 Hits Leads Pirates Past Rockies, 7–5," Associated Press, July 27, 2014, https://apnews.com/article/d20cb21899204370a6cb8df7dbd82145.

25. Frankie Frisch, "Speed to Win for Cardinals," *Los Angeles Times*, October 4, 1931: F-2.

26. Ritter, *The Glory of Their Times*, 107.

27. Dan Steinberg, "The 10 Most Embarrassing Moments in Nationals History," *Washington Post*, November 3, 2015, https://www.washingtonpost.com/news/dc-sports-bog.

28. "Champion New Yorkers Beaten at Chicago," *New York Times*, August 10, 1905: 5.

29. "Jon Tayler, "Watch: Ryan Raburn's Ghastly Error Creates Saddest Inside the Park HR," *Sports Illustrated*, July 24, 2017, https://www.si.com.

30. "Braves Victims of Freak Double Play," *Boston Globe*: April 20, 1923, 22.

31. Brian Costello, "Shea Home to Strange Double-Play," *New York Post*. October 5, 2006, https://nypost.com/2006/10/05/shea-home-to-strange-double-play/.

32. Ritter, *The Glory of Their Times*, 246–48.

33. Al Demaree, "Dugan Describes Most Peculiar Play He's Seen," *Boston Globe*, March 4, 1925, A-7.

34. "Missed Ball but Found Gold," *Pittsburgh Press*, June 25, 1905, 15.

35. "Gen. Abner Doubleday," *New York Times*, January 28, 1893, 2.

36. Daniel Steinberg, "Julian Tavaras Sounds Like a Fun Guy," *Washington Post*, March 17, 2009, https://www.voices.washingtonpost.com/dcsportsbog.

37. "The Ol' Perfesser' Taught in a Language Style, All His Own," *Washington Post*, July 30, 1990, https://www.washingtonpost.com/archive/sports/1990/07/30/the-ol-perfesser-taught-in-a-language-style-all-his-own/2f0e674c-0d21–477f-93a1-bac31f131d66/.

38. Hal Bodley, "Respected Cox Deserving of Spot in Cooperstown," MLB, December 9, 2013, https://www.mlb.com.

39. Roy Johnson, "Bobby Cox: Best of Our Generation," ESPN, July 15, 2010, https://www.espn.com.sg/espn/commentary/news/story?page=johnson/100715.

40. Larry Eldridge, "Baseball's 1982 Awards Stir Less Controversy Than Usual," *Christian Science Monitor*, December 2, 1982, https://www.csmonitor.com/1982/1202/120233.html.

41. Pat Borzi, "Elvis Andrus Leads Rangers Revolution of Savvy Over Slugging," *New York Times*, October 21, 2010, B10.

42. Bill Deane, *Baseball Myths: Debating, Debunking and Disproving Tales from the Diamond* (Lanham, MD: Scarecrow Press, 2012), 10.

43. "Ernie Shore; Pitched a Rare Perfect Game After Relieving Ruth," *New York Times*, September 26, 1980, M6.

44. Ian Hunter, "Flashback Friday: Dave Winfield Hits a Seagull," Blue Jay Hunter, September 9, 2011, http://bluejayhunter.com/2011/09/acid-flashback-friday-dave-winfield.html.

45. John Skipper, *Inside Pitch: A Closer Look at Classic Baseball Moments* (Jefferson, NC: McFarland, 1996), 142.

46. George Plimpton, "The Curious Case of Sidd Finch," *Sports Illustrated*, April 1, 1985, https://www.si.com/mlb/2014/10/15/curious-case-sidd-finch.

47. Bill James, *The New Bill James*

Historical Baseball Abstract (New York: Free Press, 2001), 158.

48. Rhiannon Walker, "The Day Hank Aaron Had a Home Run Taken Away by the Home Plate Umpire," The Undefeated, August 16, 2017, https://theundefeated.com/features/the-day-hank-aaron-had-a-home-run-taken-away-by-the-plate-umpire/.

49. Bob Uecker, and Mickey Herkovwitz, *Catcher in the Wry: Outrageous but True Stories of Baseball* (New York: Jove, 1983), 80.

50. *Ibid.*, 68.

51. Jim Bouton, *Ball Four: The Final Pitch* (North Egremont, MA: Bulldog Publishing, 2000), 294.

52. Jack O'Connell, "Loss Is a Long Story," *Hartford Courant*, May 10, 1987, C1.

53. *Ibid.*

54. "Tebbets Is Fined $50: Redleg Manager Assessed for Row with Umpire Stewart," *New York Times*, August 17, 1954.

55. Gilbert Rogin, "'Managed Good but Boy Did They Play Bad," *Sports Illustrated*, August 17, 1964, https://vault.si.com/vault/1964/08/17/i-managed-good-but-boy-did-they-play-bad.

56. Jace Evans, "Bad Misplay by Blue Jays Randal Grichuk Gives Rays Avisail Garcia Inside-the-Park Homer," *USA Today*, May 28, 2019, https://www.usatoday.com/story/sports/mlb/2019/05/28/randal-grichuk-misplay-avisail-garcia-inside-park-home-run/1266203001/.

57. Mike Klingamin, "Orioles Pitcher Billy Loes Once Lost a Grounder 'in the Sun,'" *Baltimore Sun*, July 22, 2015, https://www.baltimoresun.com/sports/orioles/bs-sp-daffy-dozen-billy-loes-0722-20150721-story.html.

58. John Drebinger, "Giants Win in 10th from Indians, 5–2, on Rhodes' Homer," *New York Times*, September 30, 1954, 1.

59. "Reminder of Gionfriddo: Dimaggio Calls Dodger's Catch Better Than May's Play," *New York Times*, September 30, 1954, 40.

60. "Mays Catch Appraised: Better Play Made By Willie in Brooklyn, Giants Scout Says," *New York Times*, September 30, 1954, 40.

61. George Vecsey, "Hazy Sunshine, Vivid Memory: The Catch 50 Years Later," *New York Times*, September 29, 2004, D-1.

62. Stark, *The Stark Truth*, 173.

63. "Henry Schulman, "Stumbling Giants Steal Win in Ninth: Murray Slips, Falls but Still Scores," SF Gate, April 5, 2001, https://www.sfgate.com.

64. Jason Turbow, "Don't Bunt to Break Up a No-Hitter," Baseball Codes, May 26, 2011, https://thebaseballcodes.com/category/dont-bunt-to-break-up-a-no-hitter/.

65. "Wolf Outpitches D-backs' Haren as Dodgers Win Early Series in Arizona," ESPN.com, April 12, 2009, https://www.espn.com/mlb/recap?gameId=290412129.

66. Bouton, *Ball Four*, 182.

67. Deane, *Baseball Myths*, 35.

68. Ritter, *The Glory of Their Times*, 46.

69. "Queer Plays in Baseball Which Have Made the Lives of Umps Sad," *Los Angeles Times*, September 11, 1911, 113.

70. Parton Keese, "4 Homers by A's Subdue Orioles, 6–3," *New York Times*, October 8, 1973, 47.

71. Associated Press, "Basepath Bungle Helps Sox," *St. Cloud Times*, May 19, 1986, 27.

72. Stephen Jay Gould, "Jim Bowie's Letter and Bill Buckner's Legs," in *Triumph and Tragedy in Mudville: A Lifelong Passion for Baseball* (New York: W.W. Norton, 2003), 235.

73. James, *The New Bill James Historical Baseball Abstract*, 891.

74. *Tampa Bay Times*, April 7, 1996, 86.

75. Larry Ruttman, *American Jews and America's Game: Voices of a Growing Legacy in Baseball* (Lincoln: University of Nebraska Press, 2013), 178.

76. Richard Vidmer, "Robins in Form, Win Two in Day," *New York Times*, August 16, 1926, 11.

77. *Ibid.*

78. Harold Kaese, "Vance, 'Late Starter': In Minors Till 31; Then Won 197 Games," *Boston Globe*, February 19, 1961, 58.

Notes

79. Ritter, *The Glory of Their Times*, 216.

80. J.P. Hoornstra, *The Fifty Greatest Dodgers Games of All Time* (Riverdale Avenue Press, 2015, 157).

81. Bill Nowlin, "Walter Carlisle," SABR Biography Project, https://www.*sabr.org/bioproj/person/walter-carlisle*.

82. Ira Berkow, "The Potato Catcher Makes His Return," *New York Times*, February 15, 1927, B15.

83. Ritter, *The Glory of Their Times*, 43–44.

84. Bob Nightengale, "Angels Are Winners in 'Who's on Third?': Baseball: Everyone looks for answers after bizarre double play ends Orioles threat in eighth inning," *Los Angeles Times*, April 18, 1993, https://www.latimes.com/archives/la-xpm-1993-04-18-sp-24330-story.html.

85. *Ibid.*

86. *Ibid.*

87. Bouton, *Ball Four*, 229.

88. Ross Newhan, "Dodgers Lose Amid Confusion, 7–3," *Los Angeles Times*, June 20, 1974, B-1.

89. Bruce Markuson, "Ted Simmons and the Bizarre Brawl," *Hardball Times*, March 17, 2020, https://tht.fangraphs.com/ted-simmons-and-the-bizarre-brawl/.

Bibliography

Books

Barra, Allen. *Clearing the Bases: The Greatest Baseball Debates of the Last Century.* Lincoln: University of Nebraska Press, 2002.

Bouton, Jim. *Ball Four: The Final Pitch.* North Egremont, MA: Bulldog, 2000.

Callahan, Tom. *Gods at Play: An Eyewitness Account of Great Moments in American Sports.* New York: W.W. Norton, 2020.

Cobb, Ty, with Al Stump. *My Life in Baseball: The True Record.* Lincoln: University of Nebraska Press, 1993.

Dawidoff, Nicholas. *The Catcher Was a Spy: The Mysterious Life of Moe Berg.* New York: Vintage, 1995.

Deane, Bill. *Baseball Myths: Debating, Debunking and Disproving Tales from the Diamond.* Lanham, MD: Scarecrow Press, 2012.

_____. *Finding the Hidden-Ball Trick: The Colorful History of Baseball's Oldest Ruse.* Lanham, MD: Rowman & Littlefield, 2015.

Frommer, Harvey. *Baseball's Greatest Managers.* Guilford, CT: Lyons Press, 1985.

Gould, Stephen Jay. "Jim Bowie's Letter and Bill Buckner's Legs." In *Triumph and Tragedy in Mudville: A Lifelong Passion for Baseball,* 219–242. New York: W.W. Norton, 2003.

Hoornstra, J.P. *The Fifty Greatest Dodgers Games of All Time.* Riverdale, NY: Riverdale Avenue, 2015.

Istorico, Ray. *Greatness in Waiting: An Illustrated History of the Early New York Yankees, 1903–1919.* Jefferson, NC: McFarland, 2013.

James, Bill. *The New Bill James Historical Baseball Abstract.* New York: Free Press, 2001.

Kurkjian, Tim. *Is This a Great Game or What? From A-Rod's Heart to Zim's Head.* New York: St. Martin's, 2007.

Lewis, Michael. *Moneyball: The Art of Winning an Unfair Game.* New York: W.W. Norton, 2004.

Okrent, Daniel, and Steve Wulf. *Baseball Anecdotes.* New York: Oxford University Press, 1989.

Prager, Joshua. *The Echoing Green: The Untold Story of Bobby Thomson, Ralph Branca and the Shot Heard Round the World.* New York: Vintage, 2008.

Ritter, Lawrence. *The Glory of Their Times: The Story of the Early Days of Baseball Told by the Men Who Played It.* New York: Perennial, 2002. First published 1966 by Macmillan.

Rosengren, John. *The Fight of Their Lives: How Juan Marichal and John Roseboro Turned Baseball's Ugliest Brawl into a Story of Forgiveness and Redemption.* Guilford, CT: Globe Pequot Press, 2014.

Ruttman, Larry. *American Jews and America's Game: Voices of a Growing Legacy in Baseball.* Lincoln: Univeristy of Nebraska Press, 2013.

Skipper, John. *Inside Pitch: A Closer Look at Classic Baseball Moments.* Jefferson, NC: McFarland, 1996.

Bibliography

Stark, Jayson. *The Stark Truth: The Most Overrated & Underrated Players in Baseball History.* Chicago: Triumph Books, 2007.

Uecker, Bob, and Mickey Herskowitz. *Catcher in the Wry: Outrageous but True Stories of Baseball.* New York: Jove Books, 1983.

Vincent, David. *Home Runs Most Wanted: The Top Ten Book of Monumental Dingers, Prodigious Swingers, and Everything Long-Ball.* Dulles, VA: Potomac, 2009.

Periodicals

Baltimore Sun
Boston Globe
Christian Science Monitor
Hartford Courant
Los Angeles Times
New York Post
New York Times
Pittsburgh Press
Sports Illustrated
Tampa Bay Times
USA Today
Washington Post

Online Sources

Baseball Codes
Baseball History Daily
Fangraphs.com
NBC Sportsworld
SB Nation
SF Gate

Index

183

Index

184

Index

185

Index

Index

Index

188

Index

Index

Index

Index

Index